Fix It Quick™

Favorite Brand Name™
KIDS' MEALS

Publications International, Ltd.
Favorite Brand Name Recipes at www.fbnr.com

Microwave Cooking: Microwave ovens vary in wattage. Use the cooking times as guidelines and check for doneness before adding more time.

Preparation/Cooking Times: Preparation times are based on the approximate amount of time required to assemble the recipe before cooking, baking, chilling or serving. These times include preparation steps such as measuring, chopping and mixing. The fact that some preparations and cooking can be done simultaneously is taken into account. Preparation of optional ingredients and serving suggestions is not included.

Contents

Snacketizers

Cheesy Quesadillas

½ pound ground beef

1 medium onion, chopped

¼ teaspoon salt

1 can (4½ ounces) chopped green chilies, drained

1 jar (1 pound 10 ounces) RAGÚ® Robusto!™ Pasta Sauce

8 (6½-inch) flour tortillas

1 tablespoon olive oil

2 cups shredded Cheddar and/or mozzarella cheese (about 8 ounces)

1. Preheat oven to 400°F. In 12-inch skillet, brown ground beef with onion and salt over medium-high heat; drain. Stir in chilies and ½ cup Ragú Pasta Sauce; set aside.

2. Meanwhile, evenly brush one side of 4 tortillas with half of the olive oil. On cookie sheets, arrange tortillas, oil-side down. Evenly top with ½ of the cheese, beef filling, then remaining cheese. Top with remaining 4 tortillas, then brush tops with remaining oil.

3. Bake 10 minutes or until cheese is melted. To serve, cut each quesadilla into 4 wedges. Serve with remaining sauce, heated.   *Makes 4 servings*

Prep Time: 10 minutes
Cook Time: 15 minutes

Cheesy Quesadillas

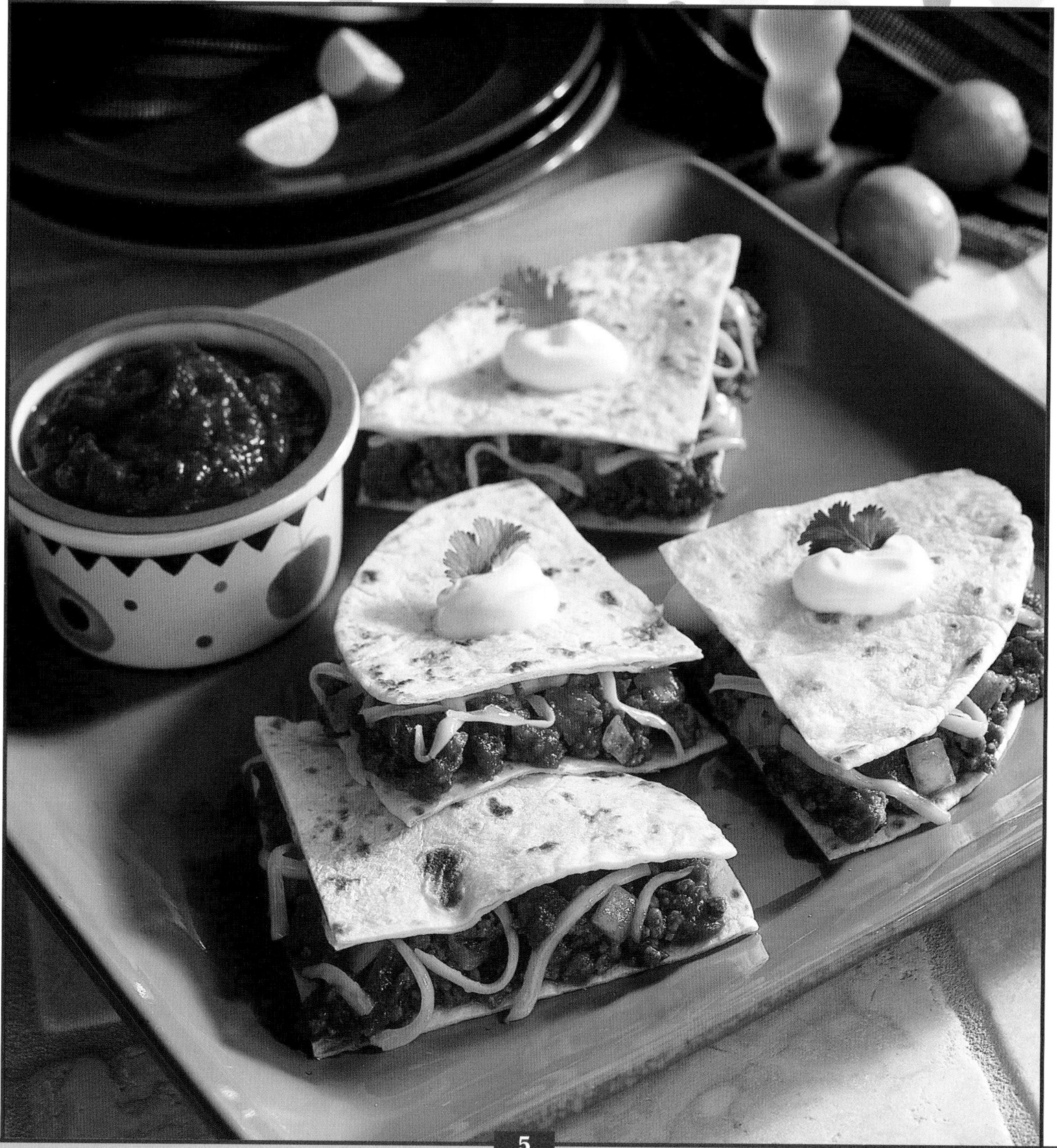

Bats' Wings with Drip Sauce

24 chicken wings (3 to 4 pounds)

1 cup low-sodium soy sauce

¾ cup unsulphured molasses

½ cup beef broth

½ teaspoon ground ginger

Drip Sauce

1 cup ketchup

2 tablespoons dark brown sugar

2 tablespoons red wine vinegar

1 tablespoon Dijon mustard

1 tablespoon sesame oil

1 teaspoon hot sauce

1. Preheat oven to 375°F.

2. Stretch out each chicken wing to resemble a bat wing. Arrange wings, skin side down, in roasting pan large enough to accommodate them in one layer.

3. Heat soy sauce, molasses, broth and ginger in small saucepan over low heat until mixture is smooth; pour evenly over wings. Bake wings 30 minutes; turn and bake 30 minutes more or until sauce is thick and sticky. Serve with Drip Sauce.

Drip Sauce

Combine all ingredients in small saucepan. Heat over medium heat until bubbly, stirring occasionally. Let cool before serving.

Makes 8 servings and 1½ cups sauce

Tuna in Crispy Won Ton Cups

18 won ton skins, each 3¼ inches square

Butter or olive oil cooking spray

1 (3-ounce) pouch of STARKIST Flavor Fresh Pouch® Albacore or Chunk Light Tuna

⅓ cup cold cooked orzo (rice-shaped pasta) or cooked rice

¼ cup southwestern ranch-style vegetable dip with jalapeños or other sour cream dip

¼ cup drained pimiento-stuffed green olives, chopped

3 tablespoons sweet pickle relish, drained

Paprika, for garnish

Parsley sprigs, for garnish

Cut won tons into circles with 3-inch round cookie cutter. Spray miniature muffin pans with cooking spray. Place one circle in each muffin cup; press to sides to mold won ton to cup. Spray each won ton with cooking spray. Bake in 350°F oven 6 to 8 minutes or until golden brown; set aside.

In small bowl, gently mix tuna, orzo, dip, olives and relish. Refrigerate filling until ready to serve. Remove won ton cups from muffin pan. Use rounded teaspoon to fill each cup; garnish with paprika and parsley.

Makes 18 servings

Tip: Cups may be made a day ahead; store in airtight container. Reheat in 350°F oven 1 to 2 minutes to recrisp.

Prep Time: 20 minutes

Bats' Wings with Drip Sauce

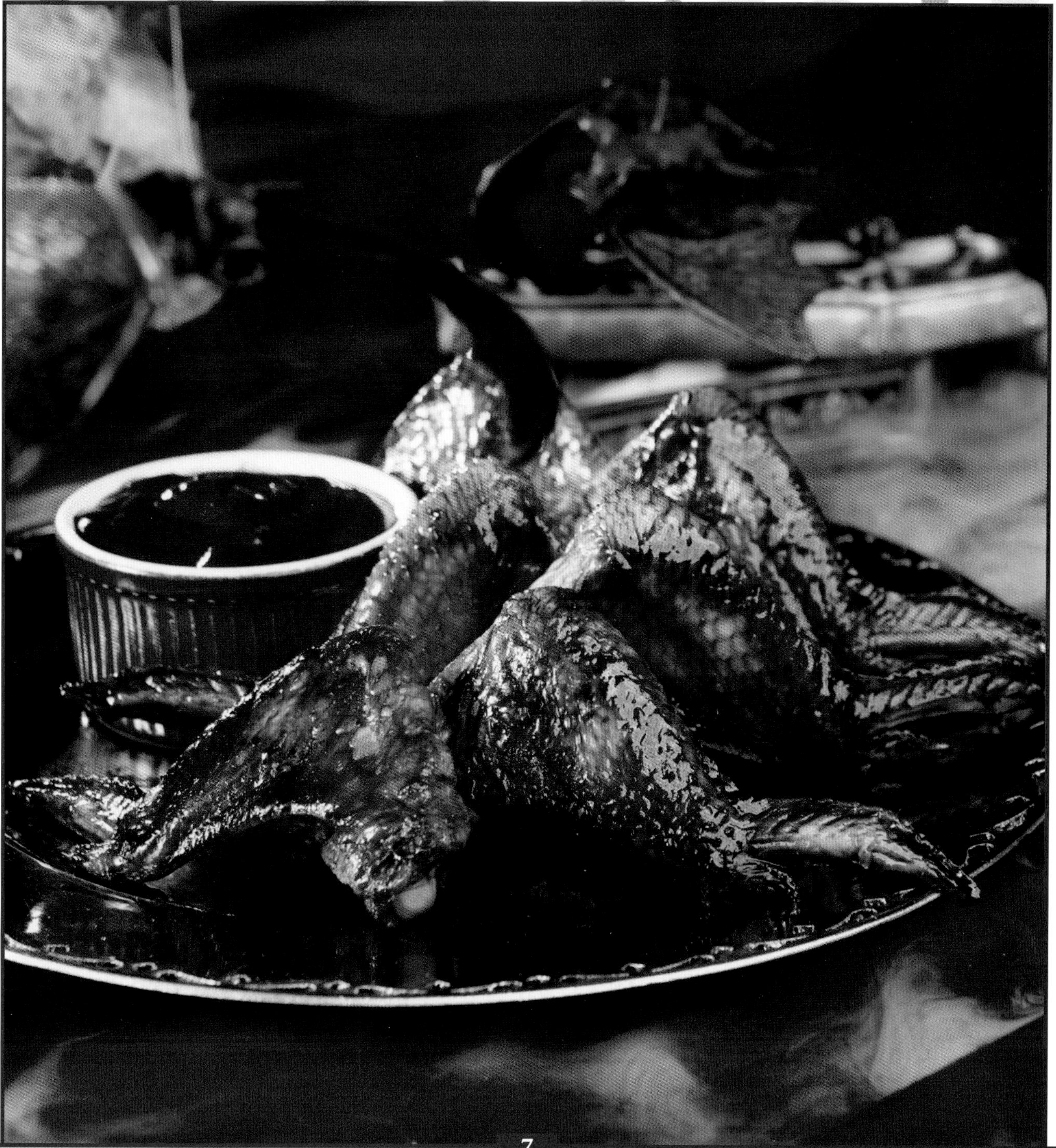

Pizza Snack Cups

1 can (12 ounces) refrigerated biscuits
    (10 biscuits)

½ pound ground beef

1 jar (14 ounces) RAGÚ® Pizza Quick®
    Sauce

½ cup shredded mozzarella cheese (about
    2 ounces)

1. Preheat oven to 375°F. In muffin pan, evenly press each biscuit in bottom and up side of each cup; chill until ready to fill.

2. In 10-inch skillet, brown ground beef over medium-high heat; drain. Stir in Ragú Pizza Quick Sauce and heat through.

3. Evenly spoon beef mixture into prepared muffin cups. Bake 15 minutes. Sprinkle with cheese and bake an additional 5 minutes or until cheese is melted and biscuits are golden. Let stand 5 minutes. Gently remove pizza cups from muffin pan and serve.

Makes 10 pizza cups

Prep Time: 10 minutes
Cook Time: 25 minutes

Eyes of Newt

2 cans (2¼ ounces each) sliced ripe olives,
    divided

¼ cup chopped roasted red pepper, divided

1 package (8 ounces) cream cheese,
    softened, divided

1 clove garlic, minced

8 (6- to 7-inch) flour tortillas

16 slices deli roast beef

1. Reserve 48 olive slices, 48 pieces red pepper and 1 tablespoon cream cheese.

2. Chop remaining olives. Combine remaining cream cheese, olives, red pepper and garlic in small bowl; mix well.

3. Spread about 2 tablespoons cream cheese mixture on each tortilla. Top each tortilla with 2 beef slices, overlapping slightly. Roll up tortillas, jelly-roll fashion. Trim off uneven ends of each tortilla roll; discard. Slice each tortilla roll into 6 (¾-inch) pieces.

4. Attach reserved olives and red pepper with reserved cream cheese to make roll-ups look like eyes.

Makes 4 dozen pieces

Tasty Tombstones

6 large baking potatoes

¼ cup olive oil

1½ tablespoons paprika

2 cups shredded Cheddar cheese

1 cup chopped black olives

1 cup chopped green onion

8 slices bacon, cooked and crumbled

1 cup ketchup or salsa

1 cup sour cream

Chopped parsley (optional)

1. Microwave potatoes on HIGH 2 minutes per potato (total time may vary according to microwave capacity). Let cool 5 minutes. Slice each potato in lengthwise into 4 slices. Heat olive oil in skillet over medium heat. Add potatoes and cook until tender and slightly browned.

2. Arrange cheese, olives, onion and bacon in rows in 13×9-inch pan or decorative dish. Place potato tombstones upright randomly throughout dish. Decorate if desired. Spoon ketchup or salsa at base of each potato. Using pastry bag or small resealable plastic food storage bag with corner removed, pipe sour cream in ghost shapes throughout dish. Sprinkle chopped parsley throughout dish to represent grass, if desired. Serve with remaining potatoes.   *Makes 6 servings*

One Potato, Two Potato

Nonstick cooking spray

2 medium baking potatoes, cut lengthwise into 4 wedges

Salt (optional)

½ cup unseasoned dry bread crumbs

2 tablespoons grated Parmesan cheese (optional)

1½ teaspoons dried oregano leaves, dill weed, Italian herbs or paprika

Spicy brown or honey mustard, ketchup or reduced-fat sour cream (optional)

1. Preheat oven to 425°F. Spray baking sheet with cooking spray; set aside.

2. Spray cut sides of potatoes generously with cooking spray; sprinkle lightly with salt, if desired.

3. Combine bread crumbs, Parmesan cheese and desired herb in shallow dish. Add potatoes; toss lightly until potatoes are generously coated with crumb mixture. Place on prepared baking sheet.

4. Bake potatoes until browned and tender, about 20 minutes. Serve warm with mustard for dipping, if desired.   *Makes 4 servings*

Potato Sweets: Omit bread crumbs, Parmesan cheese, oregano and mustard. Substitute sweet potatoes for baking potatoes. Cut and spray potatoes as directed; coat generously with desired amount of cinnamon-sugar. Bake as directed. Serve warm with peach or pineapple preserves or honey mustard for dipping. Makes 4 servings.

Tasty Tombstones

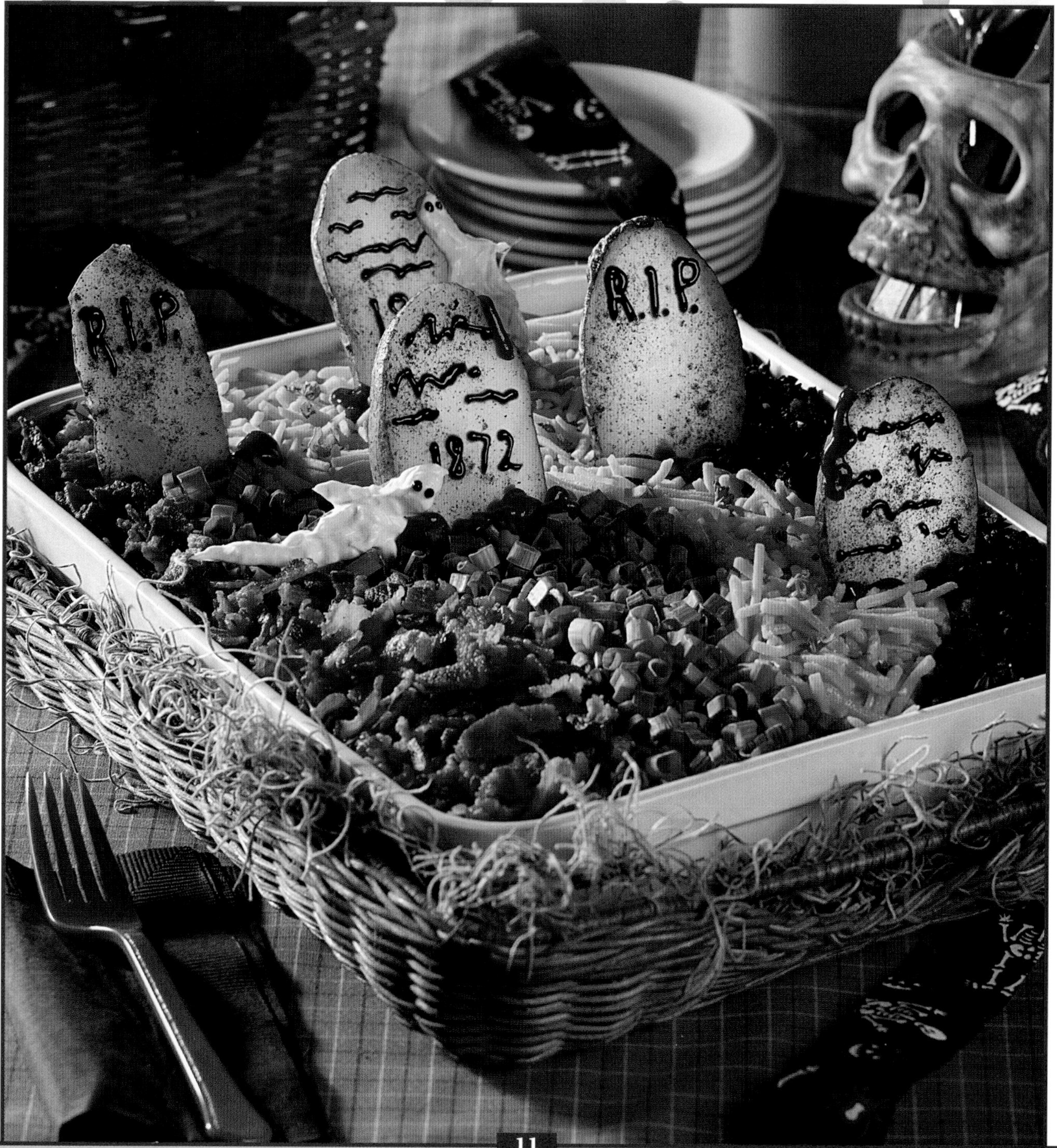

Pizza Fondue

½ pound bulk Italian sausage

1 cup chopped onion

2 jars (26 ounces each) meatless pasta sauce

4 ounces thinly sliced ham, finely chopped

1 package (3 ounces) sliced pepperoni, finely chopped

¼ teaspoon red pepper flakes

1 pound mozzarella cheese, cut into ¾-inch cubes

1 loaf Italian or French bread, cut into 1-inch cubes

Slow Cooker Directions

1. Cook sausage and onion in large skillet until sausage is browned. Drain off fat.

2. Transfer sausage mixture to slow cooker. Stir in pasta sauce, ham, pepperoni and pepper flakes. Cover; cook on LOW 3 to 4 hours.

3. Serve fondue with cheese cubes and bread cubes.   *Makes 20 to 25 appetizer servings*

Prep Time: 15 minutes
Cook Time: 3 to 4 hours

Cheese Straws

½ cup (1 stick) butter, softened

⅛ teaspoon salt

   Dash ground red pepper

1 pound sharp Cheddar cheese, shredded, at room temperature

2 cups self-rising flour

Heat oven to 350°F. In mixer bowl, beat butter, salt and pepper until creamy. Add cheese; mix well. Gradually add flour, mixing until dough begins to form a ball. Form dough into ball with hands. Fit cookie press with small star plate; fill with dough according to manufacturer's directions. Press dough onto cookie sheets in 3-inch-long strips (or desired shapes). Bake 12 minutes, just until lightly browned. Cool completely on wire rack. Store tightly covered.

Makes about 10 dozen servings

Favorite recipe from **Southeast United Dairy Industry Association, Inc.**

Dainty Digits

2 tablespoons cream cheese

24 baby carrots

24 almond slices

   Salsa

Spread small dab of cream cheese on the tip of each baby carrot. Gently press almond slice onto cream cheese to resemble fingernails. Serve on a platter with a bowl of salsa for dipping.   *Makes 4 servings*

Super Nachos

12 large baked low-fat tortilla chips (about 1½ ounces)

½ cup (2 ounces) shredded reduced-fat Cheddar cheese

¼ cup fat-free refried beans

2 tablespoons chunky salsa

Microwave Directions

Arrange chips in single layer on large microwavable plate. Sprinkle cheese evenly over chips. Spoon 1 teaspoonful beans over each chip; top with ½ teaspoonful salsa. Microwave at MEDIUM (50% power) 1½ minutes; rotate dish. Microwave an additional 1 to 1½ minutes or until cheese is melted.   *Makes 2 servings*

Conventional Directions: Substitute foil-covered baking sheet for microwavable plate. Assemble nachos on prepared baking sheet as directed above. Bake at 350°F 10 to 12 minutes or until cheese is melted.

Tip: For a single serving of nachos, arrange 6 large tortilla chips on microwavable plate; top with ¼ cup cheese, 2 tablespoons refried beans and 1 tablespoon salsa. Microwave at MEDIUM (50% power) 1 minute; rotate dish. Continue microwaving 30 seconds to 1 minute or until cheese is melted.

Guacamole Ghoul Eyes

1 ripe medium avocado

1 tablespoon minced jalapeño pepper*

1 tablespoon lime juice

¼ teaspoon garlic salt

16 cherry tomatoes

8 pitted black olives, halved horizontally

Jalapeño peppers can sting and irritate the skin; wear rubber gloves when handling peppers and do not touch eyes. Wash hands after handling.

1. Mash avocado with fork in medium bowl. Stir in jalapeño, lime juice, and garlic salt.

2. Cut off top ⅓ of each tomato. With serrated spoon, scoop out seeds; discard. Fill tomatoes with 1 rounded teaspoonful avocado mixture. Center olive half in each tomato to resemble the pupil of an eye.   *Makes 16 servings*

Cheesy Chips

10 wonton wrappers

2 tablespoons powdered American cheese or grated Parmesan cheese

2 teaspoons olive oil

⅛ teaspoon garlic powder

1. Preheat oven to 375°F. Spray baking sheet with nonstick cooking spray.

2. Diagonally cut each wonton wrapper in half, forming two triangles. Place in single layer on prepared baking sheet.

3. Combine cheese, oil and garlic powder in small bowl. Sprinkle over wonton triangles. Bake 6 to 8 minutes or until golden brown and crisp. Remove from oven. Cool completely.   *Makes 4 servings*

Super Nachos

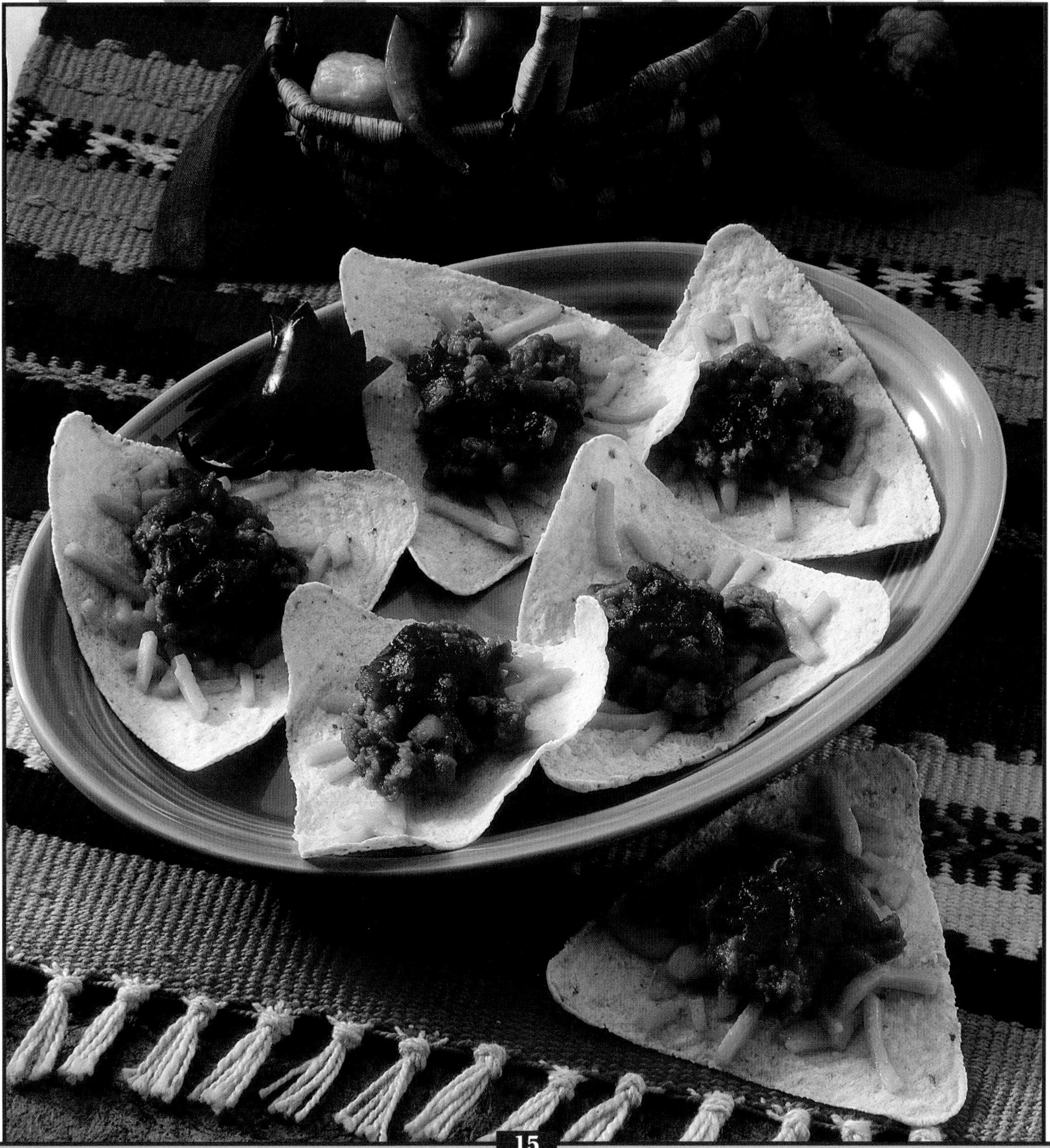

Backbones

1 package (3½ ounces) soft cheese spread with herbs

4 extra-large flour tortillas

1 bag (6 ounces) baby spinach

8 ounces thinly sliced salami or ham

8 ounces thinly sliced Havarti or Swiss cheese

1 jar (7 ounces) roasted red bell peppers, drained and sliced into strips

1. Spread 2 to 3 tablespoons cheese over each tortilla up to edge. Layer each tortilla evenly with ¼ of spinach, meat and cheese. Lay thin strips of roasted peppers down center of each tortilla.

2. Tightly roll up tortillas. Trim off and discard rounded ends of tortilla rolls.

3. Cut rolls into 1½-inch slices and secure with toothpicks. Stack 2 to 3 rolls off balance to resemble backbones. *Makes 18 servings*

Savory Pita Chips

2 whole wheat or white pita bread rounds

Nonstick olive oil cooking spray

3 tablespoons grated Parmesan cheese

1 teaspoon dried basil leaves

¼ teaspoon garlic powder

1. Preheat oven to 350°F. Line baking sheet with foil; set aside.

2. Using scissors, carefully cut each pita bread around edges to form 2 rounds. Cut each round into 6 wedges.

3. Place wedges, rough sides down, on prepared baking sheet; coat lightly with cooking spray. Turn wedges over; spray again.

4. Combine Parmesan cheese, basil and garlic powder in small bowl; sprinkle evenly over pita wedges.

5. Bake 12 to 14 minutes or until golden brown. Cool completely. *Makes 4 servings*

Cinnamon Crisps: Substitute butter-flavored cooking spray for olive oil cooking spray and 1 tablespoon sugar mixed with ¼ teaspoon ground cinnamon for Parmesan cheese, basil and garlic powder.

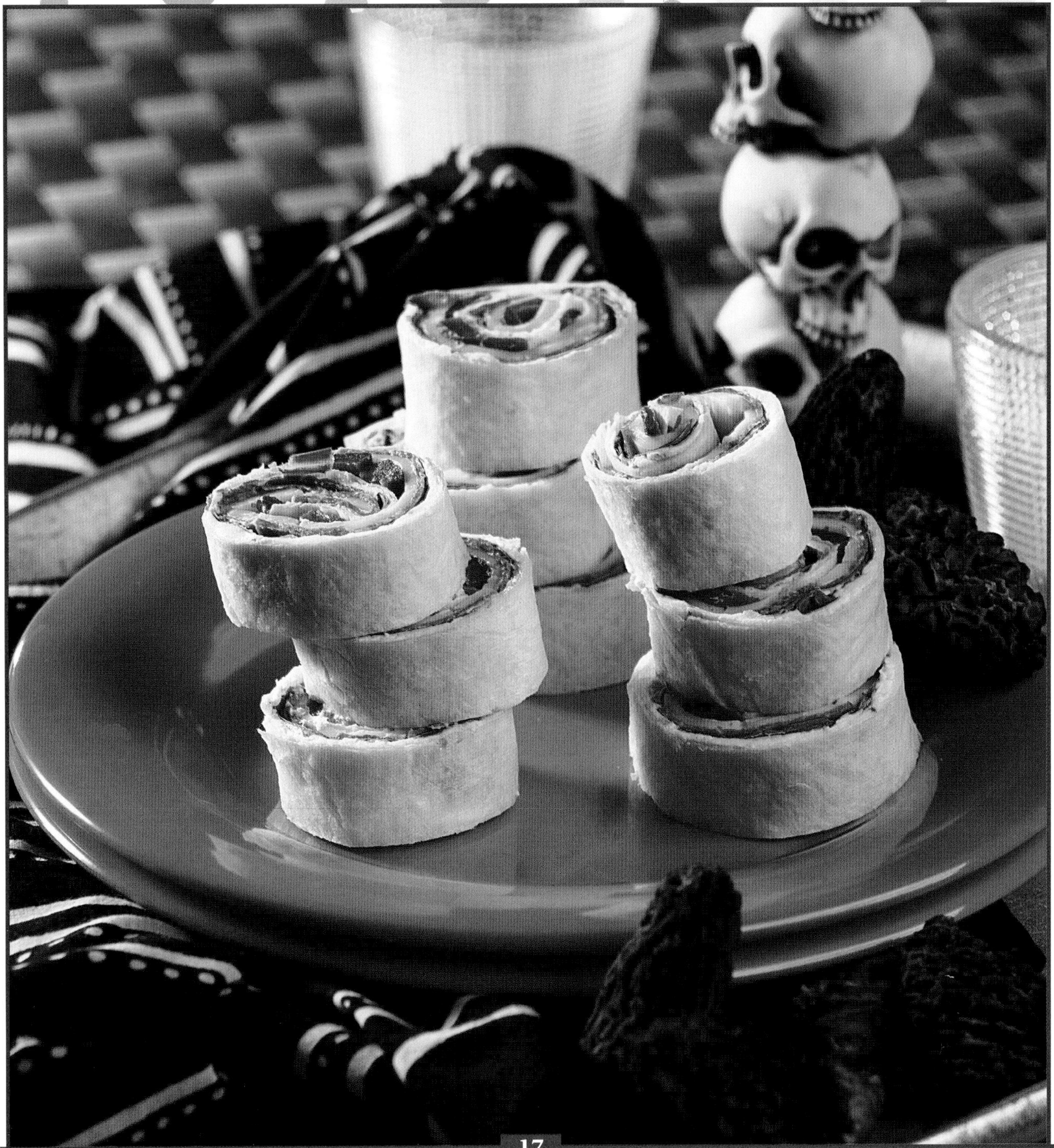

Tuna Schooners

2 (3-ounce) cans water-packed light tuna, drained

½ cup finely chopped apple

¼ cup shredded carrot

⅓ cup reduced-fat ranch salad dressing

2 English muffins, split and lightly toasted

4 triangular-shaped baked whole wheat crackers or triangular-shaped tortilla chips

1. Combine tuna, apple and carrot in medium bowl. Add salad dressing; stir to combine.

2. Spread ¼ of tuna mixture over top of each muffin half. Press 1 cracker firmly into tuna mixture on each muffin half to form "sails."

Makes 4 servings

Bat & Spook Pizzas

4 (6-inch) Italian bread shells

⅔ cup pizza or pasta sauce

1 package (3½ ounces) pepperoni slices

4 slices (1 ounce each) mozzarella cheese

1. Preheat oven to 375°F. Place bread shells on ungreased baking sheet.

2. Spread pizza sauce evenly on bread shells; top evenly with pepperoni slices.

3. Cut out ghost and bat shapes from cheese slices with cookie cutters; place on pizza sauce.

4. Bake 10 to 12 minutes or until cheese is melted.

Makes 4 servings

Pumpkin Pizzas: Spread bread shells with pizza sauce as directed. Substitute process American cheese slices for mozzarella; cut into triangles. Place cheese triangles on pizza sauce to make jack-o'-lantern faces.

Pizza Rollers

1 package (10 ounces) refrigerated pizza dough

½ cup pizza sauce

18 slices turkey pepperoni

6 sticks mozzarella cheese

1. Preheat oven to 425°F. Coat baking sheet with nonstick cooking spray.

2. Roll out pizza dough on baking sheet to form 12×9-inch rectangle. Cut dough into 6 (4½×4-inch) rectangles. Spread about 1 tablespoon sauce over center third of each rectangle. Top with 3 slices pepperoni and 1 stick of mozzarella cheese. Bring ends of dough together over cheese, pinching to seal. Place seam side down on prepared baking sheet.

3. Bake in center of oven 10 minutes or until golden brown.

Makes 6 servings

Tuna Schooners

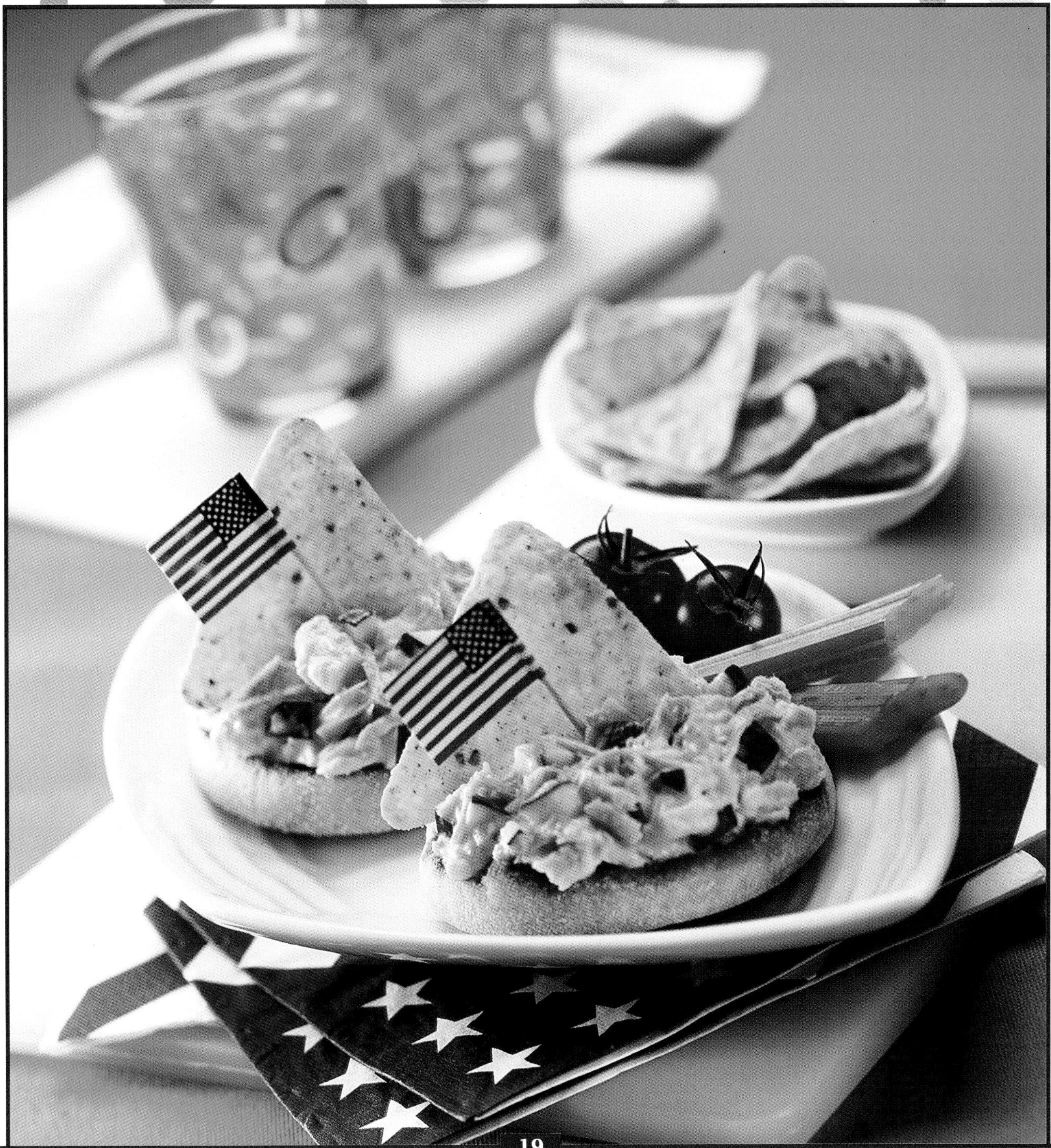

Sweet and Sour Hot Dog Bites

¼ cup prepared mustard

½ cup SMUCKER'S® Grape Jelly

1 tablespoon sweet pickle relish

½ pound frankfurters, cooked

In a saucepan, combine mustard, SMUCKER'S® jelly, and relish.

Heat over very low heat, stirring constantly, until mixture is hot and well blended.

Slice frankfurters diagonally into bite-size pieces. Add to sauce and heat thoroughly.

Makes 20 snack servings

Chicken Ranch-Up!™ Wraps

½ cup Wish-Bone® Ranch Up!™ Classic
   Light, Zesty or Classic Dressing

4 (8-inch) flour tortillas

2 cups cut-up cooked chicken

2 cups vegetables, such as: red, yellow or
   green bell peppers, red or green onion,
   cucumber, tomato, shredded carrots

Spread Ranch-Up!™ over tortillas, then top with remaining ingredients.

Roll up and serve. *Makes 4 servings*

Kid Friendly Tip: After rolling, cut the wrap on a diagonal to make 1-inch bite sized pieces.

Prep Time: 10 minutes

Abracadabra Hats

1 package crescent dinner rolls (8 rolls)

½ teaspoon dried basil leaves (optional)

16 turkey pepperoni slices

3 to 4 salami sticks, cut into 2-inch pieces

2 cups pizza or marinara sauce

1. Preheat oven to 375°F.

2. Separate dough; gently shape each piece into tall triangle. Sprinkle evenly with basil, if desired.

3. Using biscuit cutter or knife, cut pepperoni pieces into crescents. (Each slice will make two crescents). Place 1 salami stick piece along the base of each dough triangle. Roll up dough to completely cover salami, about one third of the way up. (This gives the appearance of the brim of a hat.)

4. Arrange 2 pepperoni crescents on top part of each "hat." Transfer to nonstick baking sheet. Bake 12 minutes or until slightly golden on edges. Meanwhile, warm sauce in small saucepan. Serve with "hats" for dipping.

Makes 8 servings

Sweet and Sour Hot Dog Bites

21

Confetti Tuna in Celery Sticks

1 (3-ounce) pouch of STARKIST Flavor Fresh Pouch® Albacore or Chunk Light Tuna

½ cup shredded red or green cabbage

½ cup shredded carrot

¼ cup shredded yellow squash or zucchini

3 tablespoons reduced-calorie cream cheese, softened

1 tablespoon plain low-fat yogurt

½ teaspoon dried basil, crushed

Salt and pepper to taste

10 to 12 (4-inch) celery sticks, with leaves if desired

1. In a small bowl toss together tuna, cabbage, carrot and squash.

2. Stir in cream cheese, yogurt and basil. Add salt and pepper to taste.

3. With small spatula spread mixture evenly into celery sticks. *Makes 10 to 12 servings*

Prep Time: 20 minutes

Make Your Own Pizza Shapes

1 package (10 ounces) refrigerated pizza dough

¼ to ½ cup prepared pizza sauce

1 cup shredded mozzarella cheese

1 cup *French's*® French Fried Onions

1. Preheat oven to 425°F. Unroll dough onto greased baking sheet. Press or roll dough into 12×8-inch rectangle. With sharp knife or pizza cutter, cut dough into large shape of your choice (butterfly, heart, star). Reroll scraps and cut into mini shapes.

2. Pre-bake crust 7 minutes or until crust just begins to brown. Spread with sauce and top with cheese. Bake 6 minutes or until crust is deep golden brown. Sprinkle with French Fried Onions. Bake 2 minutes longer or until golden. *Makes 4 to 6 servings*

Tip: Pizza dough can be cut with 6-inch shaped cookie cutters. Spread with sauce and top with cheese. Bake about 10 minutes or until crust is golden. Sprinkle with French Fried Onions. Bake 2 minutes longer.

Prep Time: 10 minutes
Cook Time: 15 minutes

Confetti Tuna in Celery Sticks

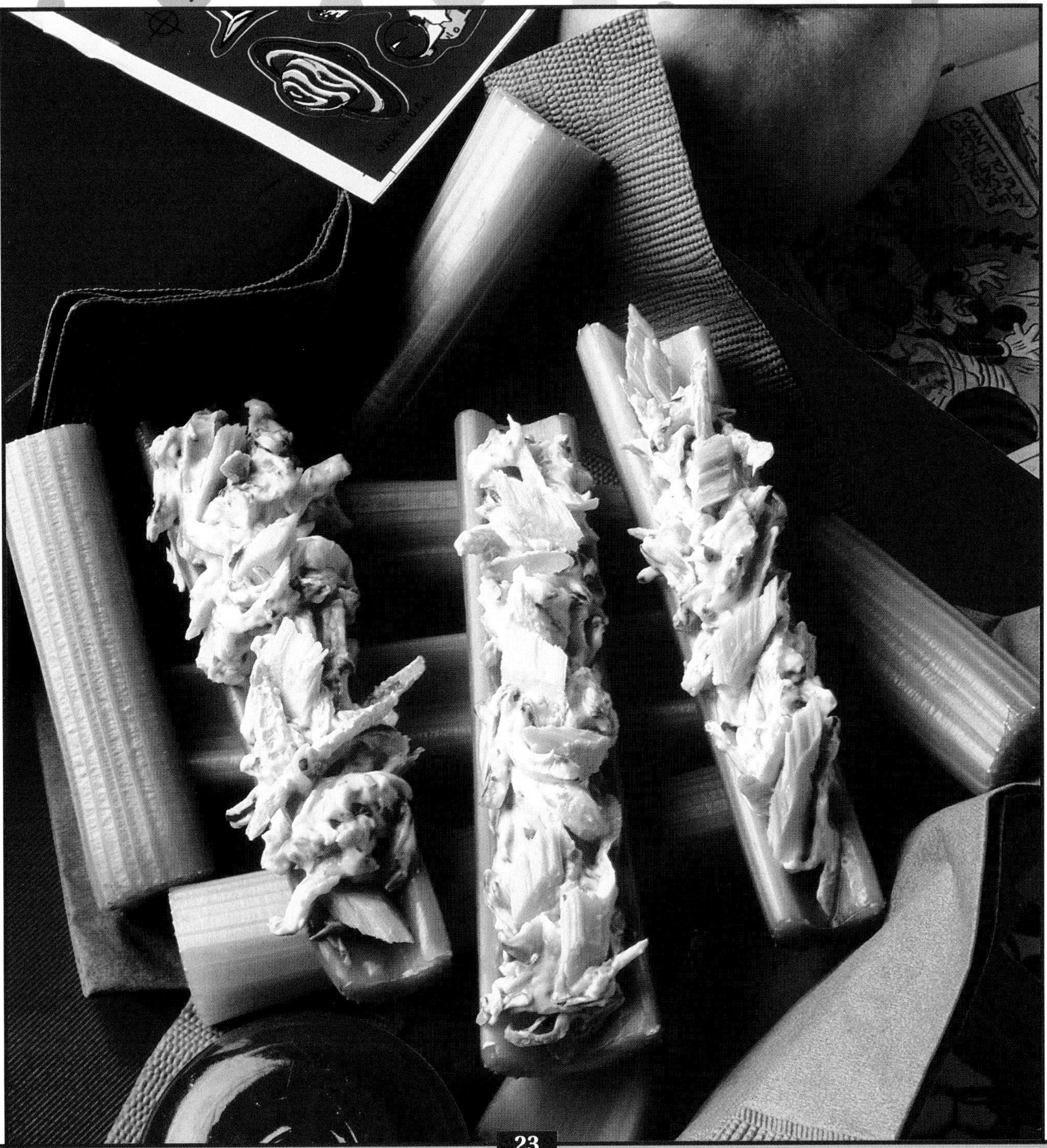

Eyeballs

12 hard-cooked eggs

1 can (4½ ounces) deviled ham

⅓ cup mayonnaise

¼ cup drained sweet pickle relish

4 teaspoons prepared mustard

12 pimiento-stuffed olives, halved

Salt and black pepper

Ketchup

1. Cut eggs lengthwise into halves. Remove yolks; place in small bowl. Mash egg yolks with fork; mix in ham, mayonnaise, pickle relish and mustard. Season to taste with salt and pepper.

2. Spoon filling into egg halves. Garnish with olive halves to make "eyeballs."

3. To make extra scary bloodshot "eyeballs," spoon ketchup into small resealable plastic food storage bag. Cut off very tiny corner of bag; drizzle ketchup over eggs.

Makes 12 servings

Prep Time: 25 minutes

Candy Corn by the Slice

1 package (10 ounces) refrigerated pizza dough

2 cups (8 ounces) shredded Cheddar cheese, divided

2 tablespoons paprika

¼ cup prepared Alfredo sauce

½ cup shredded mozzarella cheese

⅓ cup tomato sauce

1. Preheat oven to 400°F. Spray 13-inch round pizza pan with nonstick cooking spray. Press dough evenly into pan.

2. Combine 1 cup Cheddar cheese and paprika in medium bowl; stir until cheese is evenly colored. Set aside.

3. Spread Alfredo sauce in 4-inch circle in center of dough. Arrange mozzarella cheese on top of white sauce. Spread tomato sauce in 3-inch ring around center circle; top with Cheddar cheese mixture. Sprinkle remaining 1 cup Cheddar cheese over remaining dough to create 1½-inch border around edge of pizza.

4. Bake 12 to 15 minutes or until edge is lightly browned and cheese is melted. Cut into wedges to serve. *Makes 8 slices*

Eyeballs

Festive Franks

1 can (8 ounces) reduced-fat crescent roll
    dough
5½ teaspoons barbecue sauce
⅓ cup finely shredded reduced-fat sharp
    Cheddar cheese
8 fat-free hot dogs
¼ teaspoon poppy seeds (optional)
    Additional barbecue sauce (optional)

1. Preheat oven to 350°F. Spray large baking
sheet with nonstick cooking spray; set aside.

2. Unroll dough and separate into 8 triangles.
Cut each triangle in half lengthwise to make
2 triangles. Lightly spread barbecue sauce over
each triangle. Sprinkle with cheese.

3. Cut each hot dog in half; trim off rounded
ends. Place one hot dog piece at large end of
one dough triangle. Roll up jelly-roll style from
wide end. Place point-side down on prepared
baking sheet. Sprinkle with poppy seeds, if
desired. Repeat with remaining hot dog pieces
and dough.

4. Bake 13 minutes or until golden brown.
Cool 1 to 2 minutes on baking sheet. Serve
with additional barbecue sauce for dipping,
if desired. *Makes 16 servings*

Taco Tarts

1 tablespoon vegetable oil
½ cup chopped onion
½ pound ground turkey
1 clove garlic, minced
½ teaspoon dried oregano leaves
½ teaspoon chili powder
¼ teaspoon salt
1 package (15 ounces) refrigerated pie
    crusts
1 egg white
½ cup chopped tomato
½ cup taco-flavored shredded cheese

1. Preheat oven to 375°F. Lightly grease baking
sheets.

2. Heat oil in large skillet over medium heat.
Add onion and cook until tender. Add turkey;
cook until turkey is no longer pink, stirring
occasionally. Stir in garlic, oregano, chili
powder and salt; set aside.

3. Roll 1 pie crust to 14-inch diameter on
lightly floured surface. Cut out pairs of desired
shapes using 3-inch cookie cutters. Repeat
with second pie crust, rerolling dough if
necessary. Place half of shapes on prepared
baking sheets. Brush edges with egg white.
Spoon about 1 tablespoon taco mixture onto
each shape. Sprinkle with 1 teaspoon tomato
and 1 teaspoon cheese. Top with remaining
matching shapes; press edges to seal.

4. Bake 10 to 12 minutes or until golden
brown. *Makes 14 tarts*

Savory Zucchini Stix

Nonstick olive oil cooking spray

3 tablespoons seasoned dry bread crumbs

2 tablespoons grated Parmesan cheese

1 egg white

1 teaspoon reduced-fat (2%) milk

2 small zucchini (about 4 ounces each), cut lengthwise into quarters

⅓ cup pasta sauce, warmed

1. Preheat oven to 400°F. Spray baking sheet with cooking spray; set aside.

2. Combine bread crumbs and Parmesan cheese in shallow dish. Combine egg white and milk in another shallow dish; beat with fork until well blended.

3. Dip each zucchini wedge first into crumb mixture, then into egg white mixture, letting excess drip back into dish. Roll again in crumb mixture to coat.

4. Place zucchini sticks on prepared baking sheet; coat well with cooking spray. Bake 15 to 18 minutes or until golden brown. Serve with pasta sauce. *Makes 4 servings*

Mini Italian Meatballs

1 pound lean ground beef

¼ cup finely diced onion

3 teaspoons HERB-OX® beef flavored bouillon granules

½ cup Italian-style seasoned bread crumbs

1 egg, slightly beaten

¼ cup pizza sauce

1 (10¾-ounce) can Italian Herb tomato soup, undiluted

1 cup shredded mozzarella cheese

Vegetable oil, for frying

In bowl, combine ground beef, onion, bouillon, bread crumbs, egg and pizza sauce. Shape meat mixture in 48 (½-inch) meatballs. In large skillet, in a small amount of oil, brown meatballs until lightly browned on all sides. Place meatballs in a single layer in a 13×9-inch baking dish. Spoon soup over meatballs and sprinkle with cheese. Cover and bake at 350°F for 20 to 30 minutes or until meat is cooked through.   *Makes 48 servings*

Meatball Making: For 48 meatballs of equal size, shape meat mixture into an 8×6-inch rectangle on waxed paper. Cut into 1-inch squares; roll each square into a ball.

Prep Time: 30 minutes
Total Time: 1 hour, 20 minutes

Savory Zucchini Stix

Oodles of Noodles

Silly Spaghetti Casserole

8 ounces uncooked spaghetti, broken in half
¼ cup finely grated Parmesan cheese
¼ cup cholesterol-free egg substitute *or* 1 egg, beaten
¾ pound lean ground turkey or 90% lean ground beef
⅓ cup chopped onion
½ (10-ounce) package frozen cut spinach, thawed and squeezed dry
2 cups pasta sauce
¾ cup (3 ounces) shredded part-skim mozzarella cheese
1 green or yellow bell pepper, cored and seeded

1. Preheat oven to 350°F. Spray 8-inch square baking dish with nonstick cooking spray.

2. Cook spaghetti according to package directions, omitting salt and oil; drain. Return spaghetti to saucepan. Add Parmesan cheese and egg substitute; toss. Place in prepared baking dish.

3. Spray large nonstick skillet with cooking spray. Cook turkey and onion in skillet over medium-high heat until meat is lightly browned, stirring to separate meat. Drain fat from skillet. Stir in spinach and pasta sauce. Spoon on top of spaghetti mixture. Sprinkle with mozzarella cheese.

4. Use small cookie cutter to cut decorative shapes from bell pepper. Arrange on top of cheese. Cover with foil. Bake 40 to 45 minutes or until bubbling. Let stand 10 minutes. Cut into squares. *Makes 6 servings*

Silly Spaghetti Casserole

Octo-Dogs and Shells

4 hot dogs

1½ cups uncooked small shell pasta

1½ cups frozen mixed vegetables

1 cup prepared Alfredo sauce

Prepared yellow mustard in squeeze bottle

Cheese-flavored fish-shaped crackers

1. Starting 1 inch from one end of hot dog, slice hot dog vertically in half. Roll hot dog ¼ turn. Starting 1 inch from same end, slice in half vertically again, making 4 segments connected at the top. Slice each segment in half vertically, creating a total of 8 "legs." Repeat with remaining hot dogs.

2. Place hot dogs in medium saucepan; cover with water. Bring to a boil over medium-high heat. Remove from heat; set aside.

3. Prepare pasta according to package directions, stirring in vegetables during last 3 minutes of cooking time. Drain; return to pan. Stir in Alfredo sauce. Heat over low heat until heated through. Divide pasta mixture between 4 plates.

4. Drain octo-dogs. Arrange one octo-dog on top of pasta mixture on each plate. Draw faces on "heads" of octo-dogs with mustard. Sprinkle crackers over pasta.

Makes 4 servings

Crazy Chicken Skewers with Peanutty Good Noodles

¼ cup chicken broth

¼ cup creamy peanut butter

1 tablespoon soy sauce

¼ teaspoon ground ginger

1 pound boneless, skinless chicken breasts

Nonstick cooking spray

1 tablespoon margarine or butter

1 (4.9-ounce) package PASTA RONI® Homestyle Chicken Flavor

2 cups frozen Oriental-style mixed vegetables

1. In small bowl, combine chicken broth, peanut butter, soy sauce and ginger with whisk. Reserve 3 tablespoons sauce for noodles.

2. Cut chicken lengthwise into 1-inch-wide strips. Thread chicken onto 8 (6- to 8-inch) bamboo skewers. Spray large skillet with cooking spray. Add chicken; cook over medium-high heat 3 to 4 minutes on each side or until chicken is no longer pink inside. Brush chicken with remaining peanut sauce. Cook 1 minute to heat sauce. Remove from skillet; keep warm.

3. In large saucepan, bring 2 cups water and margarine to a boil. Slowly stir in pasta, vegetables and Special Seasonings. Return to a boil. Reduce heat to medium-low. Gently boil 6 to 7 minutes or until pasta is tender. Stir in reserved 3 tablespoons peanut sauce. Let stand 3 minutes before serving. Serve chicken skewers with pasta. *Makes 4 servings*

Octo-Dog and Shells

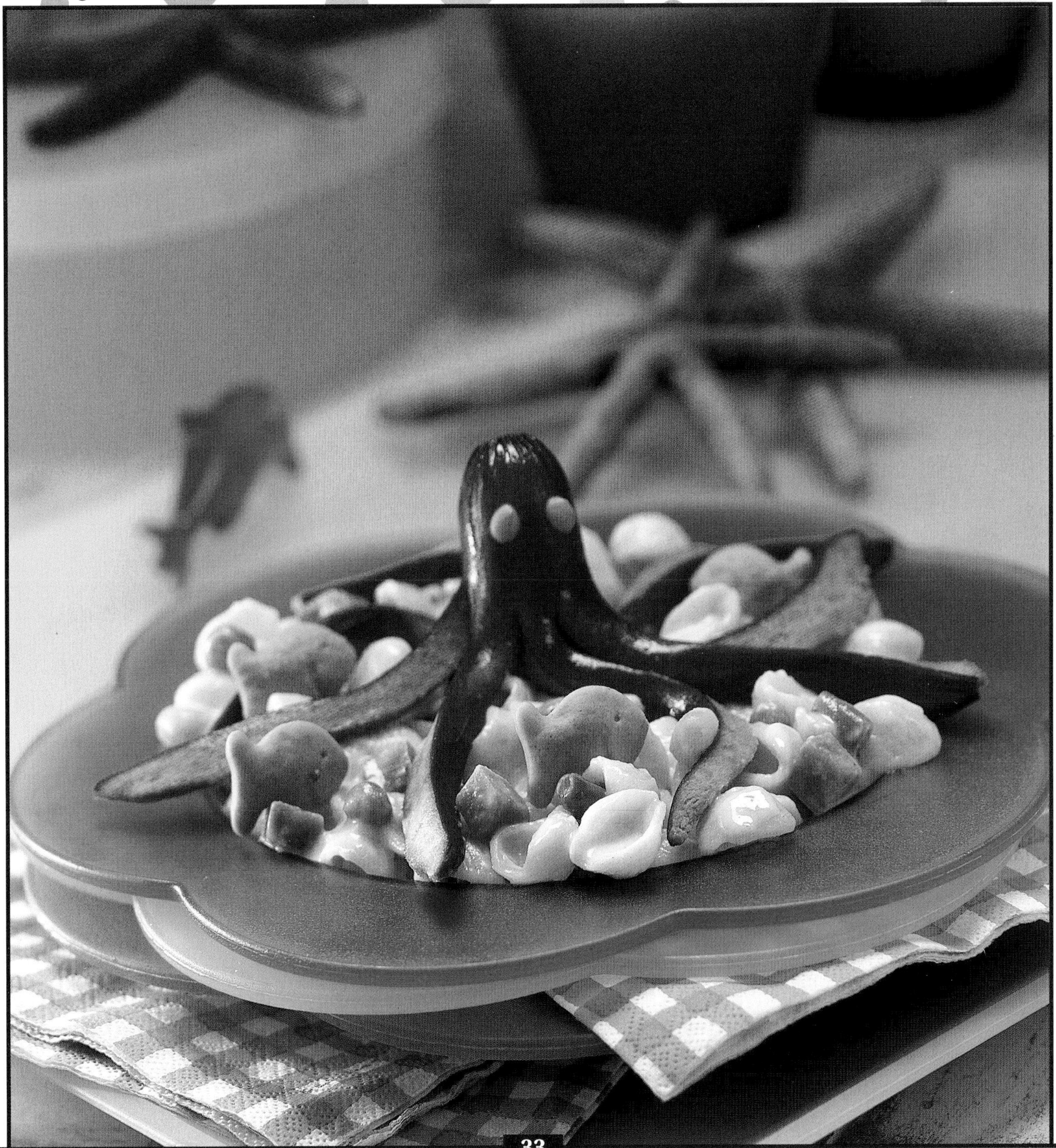

Lit'l Smokies 'n' Macaroni 'n' Cheese

1 package (7¼ ounces) macaroni and cheese mix, prepared according to package directions

1 pound HILLSHIRE FARM® Lit'l Smokies

1 can (10¾ ounces) condensed cream of celery or mushroom soup, undiluted

⅓ cup milk

1 tablespoon minced parsley (optional)

1 cup (4 ounces) shredded Cheddar cheese

Preheat oven to 350°F.

Combine prepared macaroni and cheese, Lit'l Smokies, soup, milk and parsley, if desired, in medium bowl. Pour into small greased casserole. Sprinkle Cheddar cheese over top. Bake, uncovered, 20 minutes or until heated through.   *Makes 8 servings*

Creole Macaroni and Cheese

½ cup butter or margarine

1 package (12 ounces) elbow macaroni

1 can (14½ ounces) DEL MONTE® Diced Tomatoes with Garlic & Onion

1 teaspoon salt

½ teaspoon white pepper

1 tablespoon flour

1 can (12 fluid ounces) evaporated milk

2 cups shredded sharp Cheddar cheese

1. Melt butter in large skillet. Add macaroni, tomatoes, salt and pepper. Cook 5 minutes, stirring occasionally.

2. Add 1½ cups water; bring to boil. Cover and simmer 20 minutes or until macaroni is tender.

3. Sprinkle in flour; blend well. Stir in evaporated milk and cheese. Simmer 5 minutes, stirring occasionally, until cheese is completely melted. Garnish with green pepper or parsley, if desired. Serve immediately.
Makes 4 to 6 servings

Prep & Cook Time: 35 minutes

Hot Diggity Dots & Twisters

⅔ cup milk

2 tablespoons margarine or butter

1 (4.8-ounce) package PASTA RONI® Four Cheese Flavor with Corkscrew Pasta

1½ cups frozen peas

4 hot dogs, cut into ½-inch pieces

2 teaspoons mustard

1. In large saucepan, bring 1¼ cups water, milk and margarine just to a boil.

2. Stir in pasta, peas and Special Seasonings; return to a boil. Reduce heat to medium. Gently boil uncovered, 7 to 8 minutes or until pasta is tender, stirring occasionally.

3. Stir in hot dogs and mustard. Let stand 3 to 5 minutes before serving.   *Makes 4 servings*

Prep Time: 5 minutes
Cook Time: 15 minutes

Lit'l Smokies 'n' Macaroni 'n' Cheese

Turkey and Macaroni

1 teaspoon vegetable oil

1½ pounds ground turkey

2 cans (10¾ ounces each) condensed tomato soup, undiluted

2 cups uncooked macaroni, cooked and drained

1 can (16 ounces) corn, drained

½ cup chopped onion

1 can (4 ounces) sliced mushrooms, drained

2 tablespoons ketchup

1 tablespoon mustard

Salt and black pepper

Slow Cooker Directions

1. Heat oil in large nonstick skillet over medium-high heat; brown turkey, stirring to separate meat. Transfer turkey to slow cooker.

2. Add soup, macaroni, corn, onion, mushrooms, ketchup, mustard, salt and pepper to slow cooker; mix well.

3. Cover; cook on LOW 7 to 9 hours or on HIGH 3 to 4 hours.   *Makes 4 to 6 servings*

Quick Taco Macaroni & Cheese

1 package (12 ounces) large elbow macaroni (4 cups dried pasta)

1 tablespoon LAWRY'S® Seasoned Salt

1 pound lean ground beef or turkey

1 package (1 ounce) LAWRY'S® Taco Spices & Seasonings

2 cups (8 ounces) shredded Colby longhorn cheese

2 cups (8 ounces) shredded mild cheddar cheese

2 cups milk

3 eggs, beaten

In large stockpot, boil macaroni in unsalted water just until tender. Drain and toss with Seasoned Salt. Meanwhile in medium skillet, brown ground meat; drain fat. Stir in Taco Spices & Seasonings. Spray 13×9×2-inch baking dish with nonstick cooking spray. Layer half of macaroni in bottom of dish. Top with half of cheeses. Spread taco meat over top and repeat layers of macaroni and cheeses. In medium bowl, beat together milk and eggs. Pour egg mixture over top of casserole. Bake in preheated 350°F oven for 30 to 35 minutes, until golden brown.   *Makes 6 to 8 servings*

Variation: For spicier flavor, try using LAWRY'S® Chili Spices & Seasonings or Lawry's® Hot Taco Spices & Seasonings instead of Taco Spices & Seasonings.

Prep. Time: 20 to 22 minutes
Cook Time: 30 to 35 minutes

Turkey and Macaroni

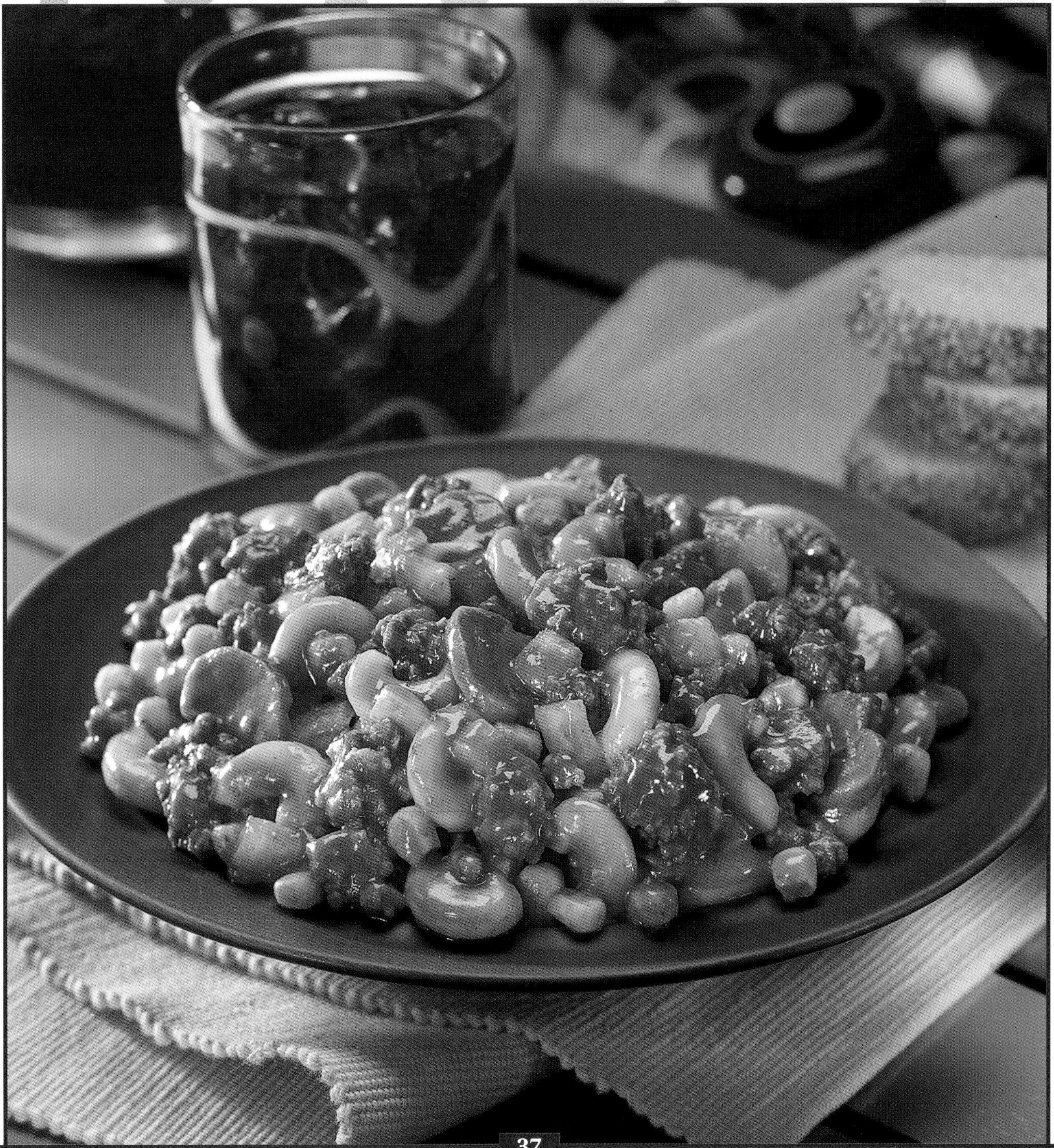

Creamy Cheese and Macaroni

1½ cups elbow macaroni

1 cup chopped onion

1 cup chopped red or green bell pepper

¾ cup chopped celery

1 cup shredded low-fat Swiss cheese

1 cup 1% low-fat cottage cheese

½ cup shredded low-fat processed American cheese

½ cup fat-free (skim) milk

3 egg whites

3 tablespoons all-purpose flour

1 tablespoon butter

¼ teaspoon black pepper

¼ teaspoon hot pepper sauce

1. Preheat oven to 350°F. Coat 2-quart casserole with nonstick cooking spray; set aside. Prepare macaroni according to package directions, omitting salt. During last 5 minutes of cooking add onion, bell pepper and celery. Drain pasta and vegetables.

2. Combine Swiss cheese, cottage cheese, American cheese, milk, egg whites, flour, butter, black pepper and pepper sauce in food processor or blender. Process until smooth. Stir cheese mixture into pasta and vegetables.

3. Pour mixture into prepared casserole. Bake, uncovered, 35 to 40 minutes or until golden brown. Let stand 10 minutes before serving.
Makes 4 servings

Skillet Spaghetti and Sausage

¼ pound mild or hot Italian sausage links, sliced

½ pound ground beef

¼ teaspoon dried oregano, crushed

4 ounces spaghetti, broken in half

1 can (14½ ounces) DEL MONTE® Diced Tomatoes with Basil, Garlic & Oregano

1 can (8 ounces) DEL MONTE® Tomato Sauce

1½ cups sliced fresh mushrooms

2 stalks celery, sliced

1. Brown sausage in large skillet over medium-high heat. Add beef and oregano; season to taste with salt and pepper, if desired.

2. Cook, stirring occasionally, until beef is browned; drain.

3. Add spaghetti, 1 cup water, undrained tomatoes, tomato sauce, mushrooms and celery. Bring to a boil, stirring occasionally. Reduce heat; cover and simmer 12 to 14 minutes or until spaghetti is tender.

4. Garnish with grated Parmesan cheese and chopped fresh parsley, if desired. Serve immediately. *Makes 4 to 6 servings*

Prep Time: 5 minutes
Cook Time: 30 minutes

Monstrous Mac & Cheese

2 packages (7 ounces each) macaroni and cheese mix

4 slices pepperoni

Pimiento-stuffed green olives

Ripe olives

Red, green and/or yellow bell peppers

1. Prepare macaroni and cheese according to package directions. Transfer to four shallow bowls.

2. Cut pepperoni, olives and peppers into strips and shapes. Arrange over macaroni for monster faces. *Makes 4 servings*

Cheesy Chicken, Coins & Strings

2 tablespoons margarine or butter

1 pound boneless, skinless chicken breasts, cut into 1-inch pieces

2 cups frozen crinkle-cut carrots

⅔ cup milk

1 (4.8-ounce) package PASTA RONI® Angel Hair Pasta with Herbs

½ cup pasteurized processed cheese, cut into ½-inch cubes

1. In large skillet over medium-high heat, melt margarine. Add chicken; sauté 5 to 7 minutes or until chicken is no longer pink inside. Remove from skillet; set aside.

2. In same skillet, bring 1⅓ cups water, carrots and milk to a boil. Stir in pasta and Special Seasonings; return to a boil. Reduce heat to medium. Gently boil uncovered, 4 to 5 minutes or until pasta is tender, stirring frequently.

3. Stir in chicken and cheese. Let stand 3 minutes or until cheese is melted.
Makes 4 servings

Prep Time: 10 minutes
Cook Time: 15 minutes

Groovy Angel Hair Goulash

1 pound lean ground beef

2 tablespoons margarine or butter

1 (4.8-ounce) package PASTA RONI® Angel Hair Pasta with Herbs

1 (14½-ounce) can diced tomatoes, undrained

1 cup frozen or canned corn, drained

1. In large skillet over medium-high heat, brown ground beef. Remove from skillet; drain. Set aside.

2. In same skillet, bring 1½ cups water and margarine to a boil.

3. Stir in pasta; cook 1 minute or just until pasta softens slightly. Stir in tomatoes, corn, beef and Special Seasonings; return to a boil. Reduce heat to medium. Gently boil uncovered, 4 to 5 minutes or until pasta is tender, stirring frequently. Let stand 3 to 5 minutes before serving. *Makes 4 servings*

Prep Time: 5 minutes
Cook Time: 15 minutes

Salsa Macaroni & Cheese

1 jar (1 pound) RAGÚ® Cheese Creations!®
  Double Cheddar Sauce

1 cup prepared mild salsa

8 ounces elbow macaroni, cooked and
  drained

1. In 2-quart saucepan, heat Ragú Cheese Creations! Sauce over medium heat. Stir in salsa; heat through.

2. Toss with hot macaroni. Serve immediately.

Makes 4 servings

Prep Time: 5 minutes
Cook Time: 15 minutes

Easy Double Cheddar
Mac & Cheese

8 ounces elbow macaroni

1 jar (1 pound) RAGÚ® Cheese Creations!®
  Double Cheddar Sauce

1. In 3-quart saucepan, cook macaroni according to package directions; drain.

2. Stir in Ragú Cheese Creations! Sauce; heat through.

Makes 4 servings

Tip: Try stirring in cut-up cooked chicken, ham or cooked broccoli florets for a great twist on the traditional.

Prep Time: 5 minutes
Cook Time: 20 minutes

Spaghetti & Meatballs

6 ounces uncooked spaghetti or vermicelli

¾ pound 95% lean ground beef or turkey

1 package (10 ounces) frozen chopped
  spinach, thawed and squeezed dry

½ cup fresh bread crumbs*

1 egg white

1 teaspoon onion powder

1 teaspoon garlic powder

½ teaspoon black pepper

  Nonstick cooking spray

2 cups pasta sauce

2 cups (5 ounces) small broccoli florets

½ cup packaged fresh julienned carrots

One small slice (½ ounce) of torn bread processed in food processor into coarse crumbs

1. Cook spaghetti according to package directions, omitting salt.

2. Meanwhile, combine beef, spinach, bread crumbs, egg white, onion powder, garlic powder and pepper in medium bowl. Mix well and shape into 32 (½-inch) meatballs.

3. Heat large deep skillet over medium heat. Coat with cooking spray. Add meatballs; cook 6 minutes, turning to brown all sides.

4. Combine pasta sauce, broccoli and carrots; pour over partially cooked meatballs. Cover; simmer over medium-low heat 12 minutes or until meatballs are cooked through and vegetables are tender.

5. Drain spaghetti; transfer to four serving plates. Top with sauce and meatballs.

Makes 4 servings

Salsa Macaroni & Cheese

Hot Dog Macaroni

1 package (8 ounces) hot dogs
1 cup uncooked corkscrew pasta
1 cup shredded Cheddar cheese
1 box (10 ounces) BIRDS EYE® frozen
   Green Peas
1 cup 1% milk

• Slice hot dogs into bite-size pieces; set aside.

• In large saucepan, cook pasta according to package directions; drain and return to saucepan.

• Stir in hot dogs, cheese, peas and milk. Cook over medium heat 10 minutes or until cheese is melted, stirring occasionally.

Makes 4 servings

Prep Time: 10 minutes
Cook Time: 20 minutes

Ham & Cheese Shells & Trees

2 tablespoons margarine or butter
1 (6.2-ounce) package PASTA RONI® Shells
   & White Cheddar
2 cups fresh or frozen chopped broccoli
⅔ cup milk
1½ cups ham or cooked turkey, cut into thin
   strips (about 6 ounces)

1. In large saucepan, bring 2 cups water and margarine to a boil.

2. Stir in pasta. Reduce heat to medium. Gently boil, uncovered, 6 minutes, stirring occasionally. Stir in broccoli; return to a boil. Boil 6 to 8 minutes or until most of water is absorbed.

3. Stir in milk, ham and Special Seasonings. Return to a boil; boil 1 to 2 minutes or until pasta is tender. Let stand 5 minutes before serving. *Makes 4 servings*

Tip: No leftovers? Ask the deli to slice a ½-inch-thick piece of ham or turkey.

Prep Time: 5 minutes
Cook Time: 20 minutes

Veggie Ravioli

2 cans (15 ounces each) ravioli
1 bag (16 ounces) BIRDS EYE® frozen
   Mixed Vegetables
2 cups shredded mozzarella cheese

• In 1½-quart microwave-safe casserole dish, combine ravioli and vegetables.

• Cover; microwave on HIGH 10 minutes, stirring halfway through cook time.

• Uncover; sprinkle with cheese. Microwave 5 minutes more or until cheese is melted.

Makes 6 servings

Serving Suggestion: Sprinkle with grated Parmesan cheese.

Prep Time: 5 minutes
Cook Time: 15 minutes

Hot Dog Macaroni

Western Wagon Wheels

1 pound lean ground beef or ground
    turkey

2 cups wagon wheel pasta, uncooked

1 can (14½ ounces) stewed tomatoes

1½ cups water

1 box (10 ounces) BIRDS EYE® frozen
    Sweet Corn

½ cup barbecue sauce

    Salt and pepper to taste

• In large skillet, cook beef over medium heat
5 minutes or until well browned.

• Stir in pasta, tomatoes, water, corn and
barbecue sauce; bring to a boil.

• Reduce heat to low; cover and simmer 15 to
20 minutes or until pasta is tender, stirring
occasionally. Season with salt and pepper.

Makes 4 servings

Serving Suggestion: Serve with corn bread or
corn muffins.

Prep Time: 5 minutes
Cook Time: 25 minutes

Tuna Starfish

8 ounces uncooked small pasta shells

1 cup crushed Cheddar cheese-flavored
    crackers

¼ cup milk

1 egg, beaten

½ teaspoon seafood seasoning blend

    Dash hot pepper sauce

    Dash Worcestershire sauce

2 cans (6 ounces each) chunk tuna packed
    in water, drained and flaked

¼ cup finely chopped red bell pepper

4 teaspoons olive oil, divided

½ cup grated Parmesan cheese

¼ cup prepared pesto sauce

    Salt and black pepper

1. Cook pasta shells according to package
directions. Drain; set aside and keep warm.

2. Combine crackers, milk, egg, seasoning, hot
pepper sauce and Worcestershire sauce in large
bowl. Add tuna and bell pepper; mix well.

3. Divide mixture into 6 balls. Flatten each ball
into ½-inch-thick patty with palm. Cut each
patty with 3-inch star-shaped cookie cutter,

4. Heat 1 teaspoon oil in medium skillet over
medium-high heat. Place 3 starfish in skillet
and cook 2 to 3 minutes or until bottoms are
lightly browned. Turn; add 1 teaspoon oil and
cook 2 to 3 minutes or until firm and lightly
browned. Repeat with remaining 3 starfish. Set
starfish aside; keep warm.

5. Combine cooked pasta, cheese and pesto
sauce. Season to taste with salt and pepper.
Serve starfish with pasta.   *Makes 3 servings*

Cheeseburger Macaroni

1 cup mostaccioli or elbow macaroni, uncooked

1 pound ground beef

1 medium onion, chopped

1 can (14½ ounces) DEL MONTE® Diced Tomatoes with Basil, Garlic & Oregano

¼ cup DEL MONTE® Tomato Ketchup

1 cup (4 ounces) shredded Cheddar cheese

1. Cook pasta according to package directions; drain.

2. Brown meat with onion in large skillet; drain. Season with salt and pepper, if desired. Stir in undrained tomatoes, ketchup and pasta; heat through.

3. Top with cheese. Garnish, if desired.

Makes 4 servings

Prep Time: 8 minutes
Cook Time: 15 minutes

Baked Pasta Casserole

1½ cups (3 ounces) uncooked wagon wheel or rotelle pasta

3 ounces 95% lean ground beef

2 tablespoons chopped onion

2 tablespoons chopped green bell pepper

1 clove garlic, minced

½ cup pasta sauce

Dash black pepper

2 tablespoons shredded Italian-style mozzarella and Parmesan cheese blend

Peperoncini (optional)

1. Preheat oven to 350°F. Cook pasta according to package directions, omitting salt; drain. Return pasta to saucepan.

2. Meanwhile, heat medium nonstick skillet over medium-high heat. Add beef, onion, bell pepper and garlic; cook and stir 3 to 4 minutes or until beef is browned and vegetables are crisp-tender. Drain.

3. Add beef mixture, pasta sauce and black pepper to pasta in saucepan; mix well. Spoon mixture into 1-quart baking dish. Sprinkle with cheese.

4. Bake 15 minutes or until heated through. Serve with peperoncini, if desired.

Makes 2 servings

Note: To make ahead, assemble casserole as directed above through step 3. Cover and refrigerate several hours or overnight. Bake, uncovered, in preheated 350°F oven 30 minutes or until heated through.

Dogs & More

Corn Dogs

8 hot dogs

8 wooden craft sticks

1 package (about 16 ounces) refrigerated grand-size corn biscuits

⅓ cup *French's*® Classic Yellow® Mustard

8 slices American cheese, cut in half

1. Preheat oven to 350°F. Insert 1 wooden craft stick halfway into each hot dog; set aside.

2. Separate biscuits. On floured board, press or roll each biscuit into a 7×4-inch oval. Spread *2 teaspoons* mustard lengthwise down center of each biscuit. Top each with 2 pieces of cheese. Place hot dog in center of biscuit. Fold top of dough over end of hot dog. Fold sides towards center enclosing hot dog. Pinch edges to seal.

3. Place corn dogs, seam-side down, on greased baking sheet. Bake 20 to 25 minutes or until golden brown. Cool slightly before serving.   *Makes 8 servings*

Tip: Corn dogs may be made without wooden craft sticks.

Prep Time: 15 minutes
Cook Time: 20 minutes

Zippity Hot Doggity Tacos

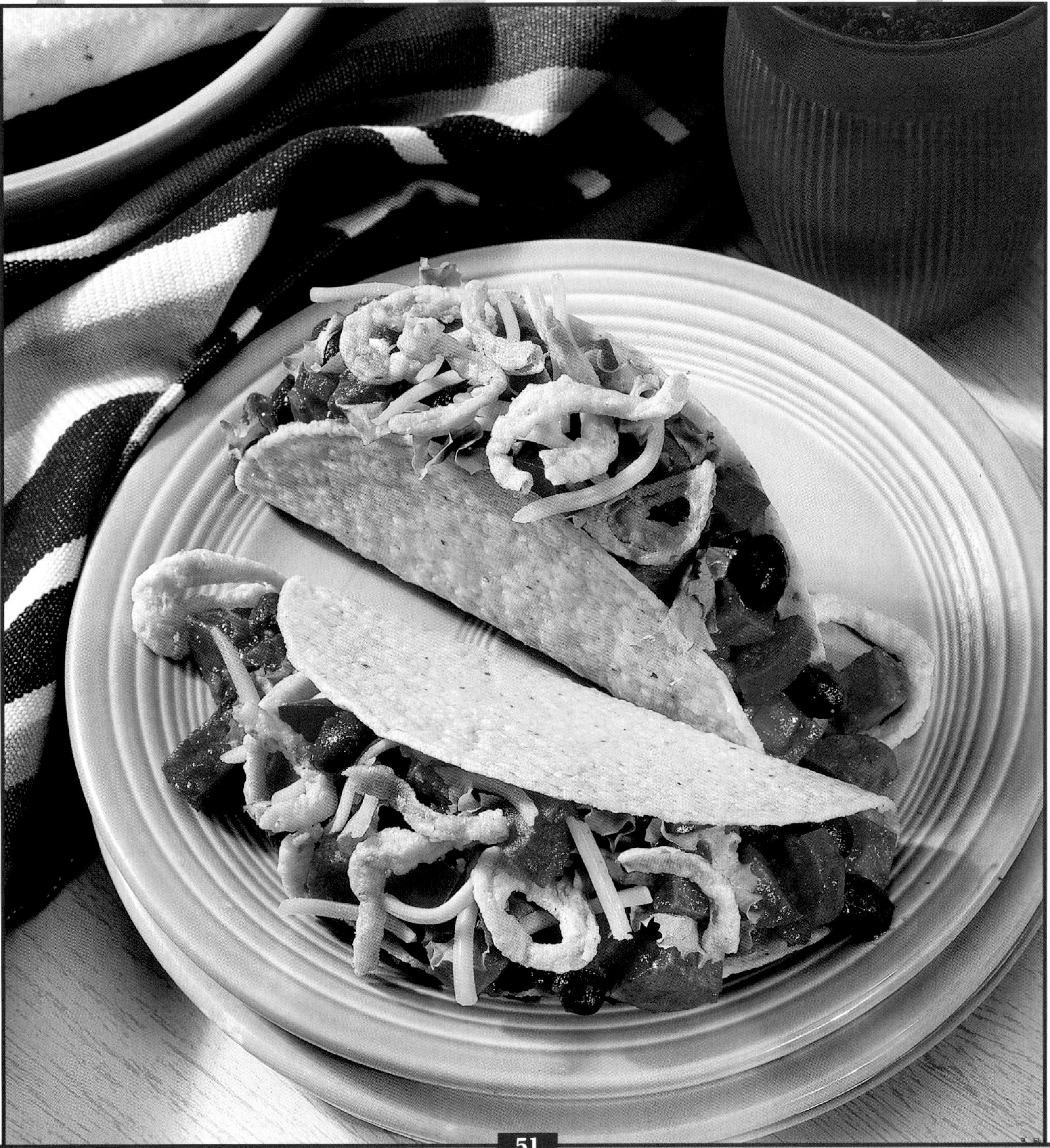

Dizzy Dogs

1 package (8 breadsticks or 11 ounces) refrigerated breadsticks

1 package (16 ounces) hot dogs (8 hot dogs)

1 egg white

Sesame and/or poppy seeds

Mustard, ketchup and barbecue sauce (optional)

1. Preheat oven to 375°F.

2. Using 1 breadstick for each, wrap hot dogs with dough in spiral pattern. Brush breadstick dough with egg white and sprinkle with sesame and/or poppy seeds. Place on ungreased baking sheet.

3. Bake 12 to 15 minutes or until light golden brown. Serve with condiments for dipping, if desired.   *Makes 8 hot dogs*

Stuffed Franks 'n' Taters

4 cups frozen hash brown potatoes, thawed

1 can (10¾ ounces) condensed cream of celery soup

1⅓ cups *French's®* French Fried Onions, divided

1 cup (4 ounces) shredded Cheddar cheese, divided

1 cup sour cream

½ teaspoon salt

¼ teaspoon pepper

6 frankfurters

Preheat oven to 400°F. In large bowl, combine potatoes, soup, ⅔ *cup* French Fried Onions, ½ *cup* cheese, sour cream and seasonings. Spread potato mixture in 12×8-inch baking dish. Split frankfurters lengthwise almost into halves. Arrange frankfurters, split-side up, along center of casserole. Bake, covered, at 400°F for 30 minutes or until heated through. Fill frankfurters with remaining cheese and ⅔ *cup* onions; bake, uncovered, 1 to 3 minutes or until onions are golden brown.

Makes 6 servings

Skillet Franks and Potatoes

3 tablespoons vegetable oil, divided

4 HEBREW NATIONAL® Quarter Pound Dinner Beef Franks or 4 Beef Knockwurst

3 cups chopped cooked red potatoes

1 cup chopped onion

1 cup chopped seeded green bell pepper or combination of green and red bell peppers

3 tablespoons chopped fresh parsley (optional)

1 teaspoon dried sage leaves

½ teaspoon salt

¼ teaspoon freshly ground black pepper

Heat 1 tablespoon oil in large nonstick skillet over medium heat. Score franks; add to skillet. Cook franks until browned. Transfer to plate; set aside.

Add remaining 2 tablespoons oil to skillet. Add potatoes, onion and bell pepper; cook and stir about 12 to 14 minutes or until potatoes are golden brown. Stir in parsley, sage, salt and pepper.

Return franks to skillet; push down into potato mixture. Cook about 5 minutes or until heated through, turning once halfway through cooking time. *Makes 4 servings*

Diggity Dog Biscuits

3 cups dry biscuit mix

1 can (15 ounces) VEG•ALL® Original Mixed Vegetables, drained and mashed

⅓ cup whole milk

2 hot dogs, chopped

½ cup shredded mild cheddar cheese

¼ teaspoon garlic salt

1 tablespoon chopped fresh parsley

Preheat oven to 400°F.

Combine all ingredients into a large mixing bowl and stir until mixture forms a moist dough.

Drop about ⅓ cup of dough at a time onto a greased cookie sheet. Pat down lightly with the back of a spoon.

Bake for 10 to 15 minutes or until golden brown. Remove and let cool for 5 minutes. Serve. *Makes 12 biscuits*

Tip: These biscuits are a great way to get kids to eat vegetables without them knowing it. Serve biscuits with butter or ketchup.

Dem Bones

1 package (6 ounces) sliced ham

¾ cup (3 ounces) shredded Swiss cheese

½ cup mayonnaise

1 tablespoon sweet pickle relish

½ teaspoon mustard

¼ teaspoon black pepper

6 slices white bread

1. Place ham in bowl of food processor or blender; process until ground. Combine ham, cheese, mayonnaise, relish, mustard and pepper in small bowl until well blended.

2. Cut out 12 bone shapes from bread using 3½-inch bone-shaped cookie cutter or sharp knife. Spread half of "bones" with 2 tablespoons ham mixture; top with remaining "bones."   *Makes 6 sandwiches*

Hot Diggity Dogs

2 tablespoons butter or margarine

2 large (1 pound) sweet onions, thinly sliced

½ cup *French's*® Classic Yellow® Mustard

½ cup ketchup

10 frankfurters

10 frankfurter buns

Melt butter in medium skillet over medium heat. Add onion; cook 10 minutes or until very tender, stirring often. Stir in mustard and ketchup. Cook over low heat 2 minutes, stirring often.

Place frankfurters and buns on grid. Grill over medium coals 5 minutes or until frankfurters are browned and buns are toasted, turning once. To serve, spoon onion mixture into buns; top each with 1 frankfurter.
          Makes 10 servings (about 2½ cups)

Tip: Onion topping is also great on hamburgers or smoked sausage heros.

Prep Time: 5 minutes
Cook Time: 20 minutes

Mummy Dogs

1 can (11 ounces) refrigerated breadstick dough (8 breadsticks)
1 package (16 ounces) hot dogs
Mustard and poppy seeds

1. Preheat oven to 375°F. Using 1 dough strip for each, wrap hot dogs to look like mummies, leaving opening for eyes. Place on ungreased baking sheet.

2. Bake 12 to 15 minutes or until light golden brown.

3. Place dots of mustard and poppy seeds for eyes.   *Makes 8 servings*

Mini Mummy Dogs: Use 1 package (16 ounces) mini hot dogs instead of regular hot dogs. Cut each breadstick strip into 3 pieces. Cut each piece in half lengthwise. Using 1 strip of dough for each, wrap and bake mini hot dogs as directed above.

Maple Francheezies

Mustard Spread (recipe follows)
¼ cup maple syrup
2 teaspoons garlic powder
1 teaspoon black pepper
½ teaspoon ground nutmeg
4 slices bacon
4 jumbo hot dogs
4 hot dog buns, split
½ cup (2 ounces) shredded Cheddar cheese

1. Prepare Mustard Spread; set aside.

2. Prepare grill for direct cooking.

3. Combine maple syrup, garlic powder, pepper and nutmeg in small bowl. Brush syrup mixture onto bacon slices. Wrap 1 slice bacon around each hot dog.

4. Brush hot dogs with remaining syrup mixture. Place hot dogs on grid. Grill, covered, over medium-high heat 8 minutes or until bacon is crisp and hot dogs are heated through, turning halfway through grilling time. Place hot dogs in buns, top with Mustard Spread and cheese.   *Makes 4 servings*

Mustard Spread

½ cup prepared yellow mustard
1 tablespoon finely chopped onion
1 tablespoon diced tomato
1 tablespoon chopped fresh parsley
1 teaspoon garlic powder
½ teaspoon black pepper

Combine all ingredients in small bowl; mix well.   *Makes about ¾ cup*

Mummy Dogs

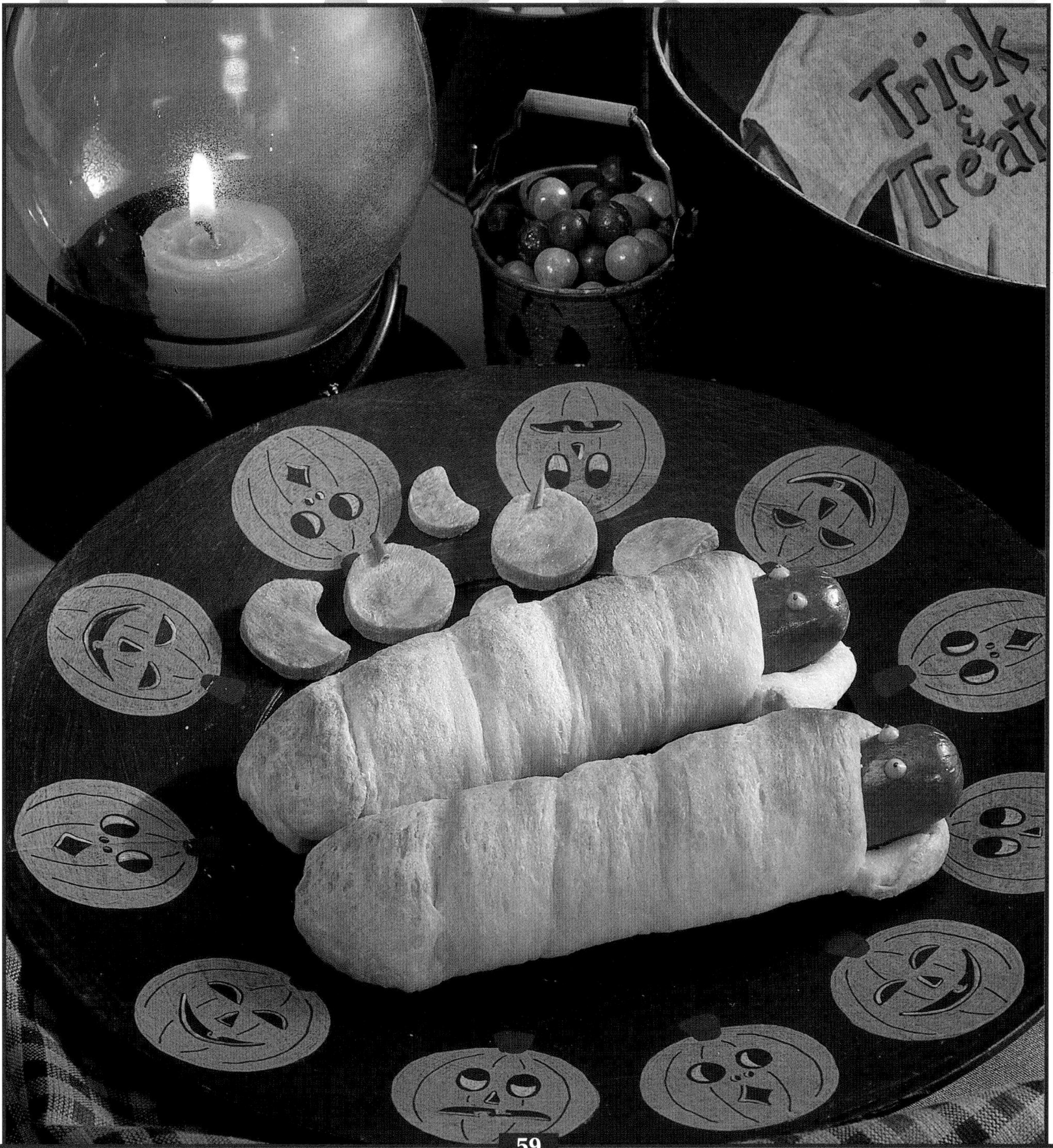

Jack-O'-Lantern Chili Cups

2 cans (11.5 ounces each) refrigerated corn breadstick dough (8 breadsticks each) *or* 3 cans (4.5 ounces each) refrigerated buttermilk biscuits (6 biscuits each)

1 can (15 ounces) mild chili with beans

1 cup frozen corn

6 slices Cheddar cheese

Olive slices, bell pepper and carrot pieces for decoration

1. Preheat oven to 425°F. Lightly grease 16 to 18 standard (2½-inch) muffin pan cups. Lightly roll out corn bread dough to press together perforations. Cut out 16 to 18 circles with 3-inch round cookie cutter. Press 1 circle onto bottom and 1 inch up side of each muffin cup.

2. Combine chili and corn in medium bowl. Fill each muffin cup with 1 tablespoon chili. Cut out 16 to 18 circles from cheese with 2-inch round cookie cutter; place rounds over chili mixture in cups. Decorate cheese with olive, bell pepper and carrot pieces to resemble jack-o'-lanterns. Bake 10 to 12 minutes or until corn bread is completely baked and cheese is melted.

Makes about 8 servings

Monterey Ranch Ham Sandwiches

4 (½-inch-thick) slices CURE 81® ham

¼ cup ranch salad dressing

4 Kaiser rolls, split

4 (1-ounce) slices Monterey Jack cheese

8 slices HORMEL® BLACK LABEL® bacon, cooked

½ cup shredded lettuce

1 tomato, thinly sliced

Broil ham slices 6 inches from heat source 5 to 6 minutes, turning once until golden brown. Spread dressing on cut sides of rolls. Layer ham, cheese, 2 bacon strips, lettuce and tomato slices on roll bottom. Cover with roll top.

Makes 4 servings

Dogs & More

Jack-O'-Lantern Chili Cups

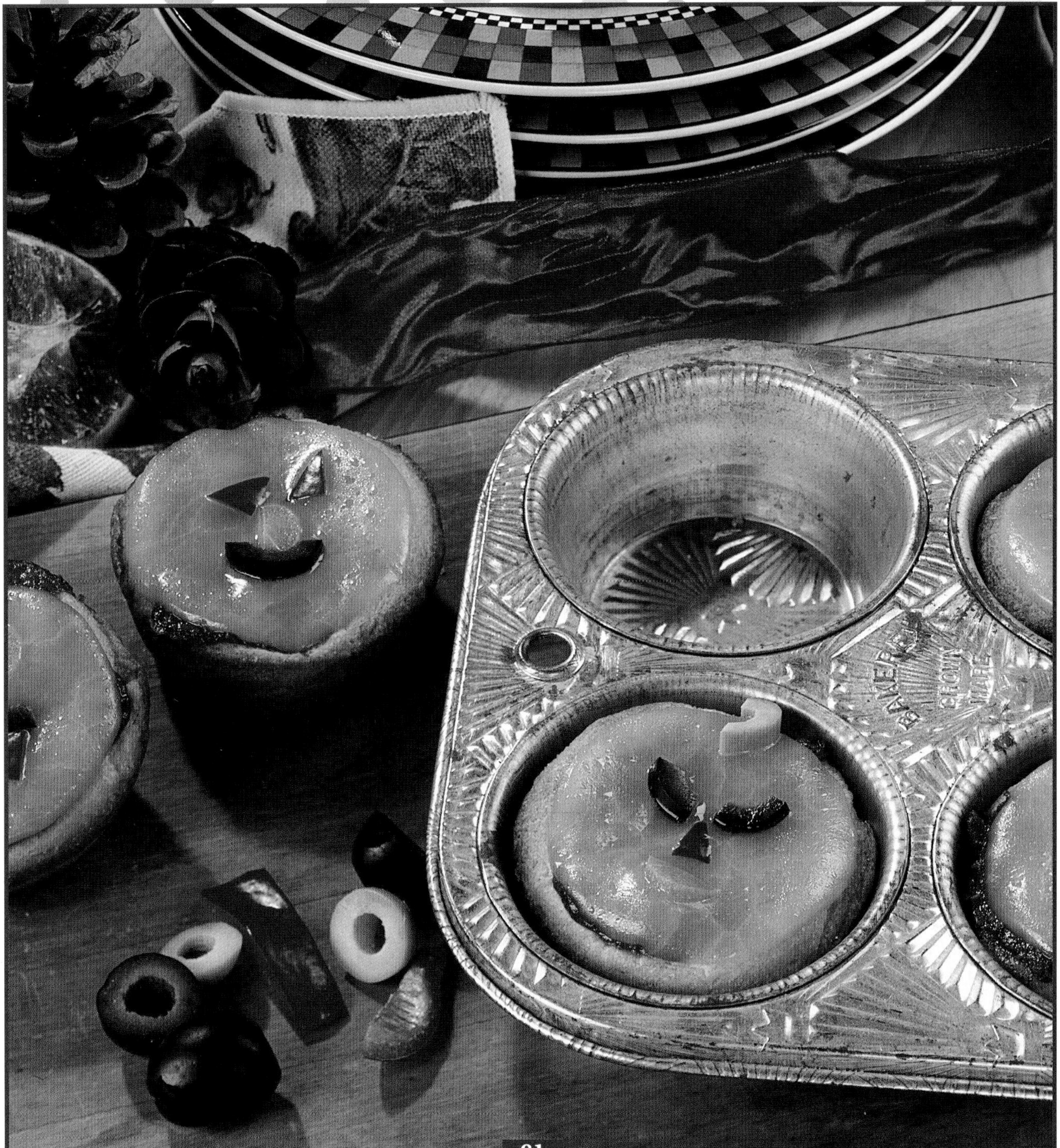

Sandwiches

Grilled Cheese & Turkey Shapes

8 slices seedless rye or sourdough bread

8 teaspoons *French's*® Mustard, any flavor

8 slices deli roast turkey

4 slices American cheese

2 tablespoons butter or margarine, softened

1. Spread *1 teaspoon* mustard on each slice of bread. Arrange turkey and cheese on half of the bread slices, dividing evenly. Cover with top halves of bread.

2. Cut out sandwich shapes using choice of cookie cutters. Place cookie cutter on top of sandwich; press down firmly. Remove excess trimmings.

3. Spread butter on both sides of sandwich. Heat large nonstick skillet over medium heat. Cook sandwiches 1 minute per side or until bread is golden and cheese melts.

Makes 4 sandwiches

Tip: Use 2½-inch star, heart, teddy bear or flower-shaped cookie cutters.

Prep Time: 15 minutes
Cook Time: 2 minutes

Sea Serpents

1 package crescent dinner rolls (8 rolls)
  Fruit-flavored ring-shaped cereal
1 egg, beaten
  Sunflower seeds, sesame seeds or poppy seeds
1 can (6 ounces) water-packed tuna, drained
  Mayonnaise
  Parsley and pimiento strips (optional)

1. Separate dough into triangles. Press each triangle into serpent shape, with thin tapered tail and wider head, on baking sheet. Head should be about ¼-inch thick.

2. Press cereal rings onto head for eyes. Brush dough serpents with egg and sprinkle with choice of seeds. Bake according to package directions.

3. When cooled, slice head end lengthwise to form a mouth. Mix tuna with mayonnaise to taste and fill mouth with tuna mixture. Add sprigs of parsley for seaweed and pimiento strips for tongues, if desired.

Makes 8 servings

Variation: If your kids don't eat tuna, fill the mouths of these hungry creatures with peanut butter, egg salad, chicken salad, or even their favorite cold cuts cut into strips.

Magnificent Salsa Meatball Hoagies

1 (6.8-ounce) package RICE-A-RONI® Beef Flavor
1 pound ground beef
½ cup dry bread crumbs
1 (24-ounce) jar salsa, divided
1 large egg
6 hoagie or French rolls, split in half
  Grated Parmesan cheese (optional)

1. In large bowl, combine rice-vermicelli mix, ground beef, bread crumbs, ½ cup salsa, egg and Special Seasonings. Shape meat mixture into 24 (1½-inch) meatballs. Arrange in large skillet.

2. Add 1½ cups water and remaining salsa; bring to a boil. Reduce heat to medium. Cover; simmer 30 to 35 minutes or until rice in meatballs is tender.

3. Place 4 meatballs in each roll. Top with sauce and cheese, if desired.

Makes 6 servings

Tip: For an Italian flair, use spaghetti sauce instead of salsa.

Prep Time: 15 minutes
Cook Time: 35 minutes

Peanut Butter and Jelly Pizza Sandwich

1 English muffin

2 tablespoons JIF® Creamy Peanut Butter

2 tablespoons SMUCKER'S® Strawberry Jam

6 to 8 slices banana

Chocolate syrup

Sweetened, flaked coconut (optional)

1. Split and toast English muffin. Spread JIF® peanut butter on both sides of the English muffin. Spread SMUCKER'S® Strawberry Jam on JIF® peanut butter.

2. Top with banana slices. Drizzle on chocolate syrup to taste. Sprinkle with coconut flakes if desired. Eat while still warm.

Makes 1 serving

Inside-Out Turkey Sandwiches

2 tablespoons fat-free cream cheese

2 tablespoons pasteurized process cheese spread

2 teaspoons chopped green onion tops

1 teaspoon prepared mustard

12 thin round slices fat-free turkey breast or smoked turkey breast

4 large pretzel logs or unsalted breadsticks

1. Combine cream cheese, process cheese spread, green onion and mustard in small bowl; mix well.

2. Arrange 3 turkey slices on large sheet of plastic wrap, overlapping slices in center. Spread ¼ of cream cheese mixture evenly onto turkey slices, covering slices completely. Place 1 pretzel at bottom edge of turkey slices; roll up turkey around pretzel. (Be sure to keep all 3 turkey slices together as you roll them around pretzel.)

3. Repeat with remaining ingredients.

Makes 4 servings

Melted SPAM® & Cheese Poppy Seed Sandwiches

½ cup butter or margarine, softened

3 tablespoons prepared mustard

1 tablespoon poppy seeds

8 slices cracked wheat bread

1 (12-ounce) can SPAM® Classic, cut into 8 slices

4 (1-ounce) slices American cheese

Heat oven to 375°F. In small bowl, combine butter, mustard and poppy seeds. Spread butter mixture on bread slices. Place 2 slices of SPAM® on each of 4 bread slices. Top SPAM® with 1 slice of cheese. Top with remaining 4 bread slices. Wrap sandwiches in foil. Bake 10 to 15 minutes or until cheese is melted.

Makes 4 servings

Peanut Butter and Jelly Pizza Sandwich

Sloppy Goblins

1 pound 90% lean ground beef

1 cup chopped onion

5 hot dogs, cut into ½-inch pieces

½ cup ketchup

¼ cup chopped dill pickle

¼ cup honey

¼ cup tomato paste

¼ cup mustard

2 teaspoons cider vinegar

1 teaspoon Worcestershire sauce

8 hamburger buns

Garnishes: Green olives, ripe olives, banana pepper slices, carrot curls and crinkles, red pepper, parsley sprigs and pretzel sticks

1. Cook beef and onion in large skillet over medium heat until beef is brown and onion is tender; drain. Stir in remaining ingredients except buns and garnishes. Cook, covered, 5 minutes or until heated through.

2. Spoon meat mixture onto bottoms of buns; cover with tops of buns. Create goblin faces with garnishes. *Makes 8 servings*

Tuna Supper Sandwiches

2 cups shredded Cheddar cheese

⅓ cup chopped green onions, including tops

⅓ cup chopped red bell pepper

1 can (2¼ ounces) sliced ripe olives, drained

2 tablespoons minced fresh parsley

1 teaspoon curry powder

Seasoned salt to taste

1 (7-ounce) pouch of STARKIST Flavor Fresh Pouch® Albacore or Chunk Light Tuna

½ cup light mayonnaise

6 soft French rolls (7 inches *each*), halved lengthwise

In medium bowl, place cheese, onions, red pepper, olives, parsley, curry powder and salt; mix lightly. Add tuna and mayonnaise; toss lightly with fork. Cover baking sheet with foil; place rolls on foil. Spread about ⅓ cup mixture on each half. Bake in 450°F oven 10 to 12 minutes or until tops are bubbling and beginning to brown. Cool slightly before serving. *Makes 12 servings*

Prep Time: 18 minutes
Cook Time: 12 minutes

Sloppy Goblin

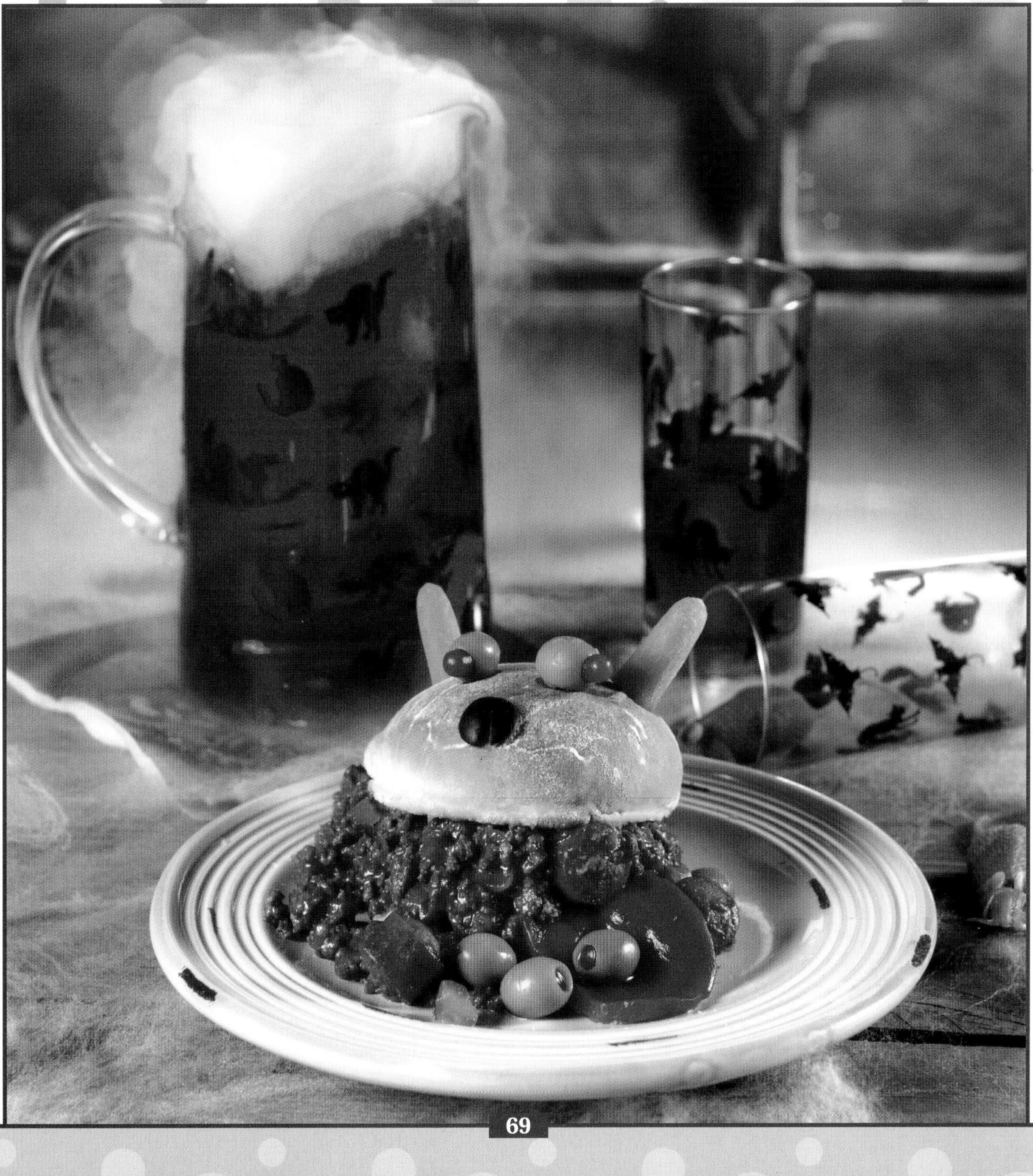

Baseball Sandwich

1 (1-pound) round sourdough or white bread loaf

2 cups mayonnaise or salad dressing, divided

¼ pound thinly sliced roast beef

1 slice (about 1 ounce) provolone or Swiss cheese

3 tablespoons roasted red peppers, well drained

3 tablespoons spicy mustard, divided

¼ pound thinly sliced ham

1 slice (about 1 ounce) Cheddar cheese

3 tablespoons dill pickle slices

2 tablespoons thinly sliced onion

   Red food coloring

1. Cut thin slice off top of bread loaf; set aside. With serrated knife, cut around sides of bread, leaving ¼-inch-thick bread shell. Lift out center portion of bread; horizontally cut removed bread round into 3 slices of equal thickness.

2. Spread 1 tablespoon mayonnaise onto bottom of hollowed out loaf; top with layers of roast beef and provolone cheese. Cover with bottom bread slice and red peppers.

3. Spread top of middle bread slice with ½ of mustard; place over peppers. Top with layers of ham and Cheddar cheese. Spread remaining bread slice with remaining mustard; place over ham and Cheddar cheese. Top with pickles and onion. Replace top of bread loaf.

4. Reserve ⅓ cup mayonnaise; set aside. Frost outside of entire loaf of bread with remaining mayonnaise. Color reserved ⅓ cup mayonnaise with red food coloring; spoon into pastry bag fitted with writing tip. Pipe red mayonnaise onto bread to resemble stitches on baseball.   *Makes 6 to 8 servings*

SPAM™ Grilled Cheese Heroes

4 (1-ounce) slices Swiss cheese

2 plum tomatoes, thinly sliced

8 slices Italian bread

1 (12-ounce) can SPAM® Classic, thinly sliced

¼ cup Dijon mustard

¼ cup thinly sliced green onions

4 (1-ounce) slices American cheese

2 tablespoons butter or margarine

Layer cheese and tomatoes evenly over 4 bread slices. Place SPAM® over tomatoes. Spread mustard on SPAM®. Sprinkle with onions. Top with American cheese and remaining 4 bread slices. In large skillet or griddle over medium heat, melt butter. Add sandwiches and cook until cheese is melted and sides are golden brown. Serve immediately.   *Makes 4 servings*

Baseball Sandwich

71

Tacos Olé

1 pound ground beef or turkey

1 cup salsa

¼ cup *Frank's® RedHot® Original Cayenne Pepper Sauce*

2 teaspoons chili powder

8 taco shells, heated

Garnish: chopped tomatoes, shredded lettuce, sliced olives, sour cream, shredded cheese

1. Cook beef in skillet over medium-high heat 5 minutes or until browned, stirring to separate meat; drain. Stir in salsa, **Frank's RedHot** Sauce and chili powder. Heat to boiling. Reduce heat to medium-low. Cook 5 minutes, stirring often.

2. To serve, spoon meat mixture into taco shells. Splash on more **Frank's RedHot** Sauce to taste. Garnish as desired.

Makes 4 servings

Prep Time: 5 minutes
Cook Time: 10 minutes

Silly Snake Sandwich

½ cup peanut butter

1 loaf (½ pound) sliced French or Italian bread, about 11 inches long and 3 inches wide

1 each red bell pepper, black olive, green olive

½ cup jelly, any flavor

¼ cup marshmallow creme

1. Using small amount of peanut butter, attach first 2 inches (3 to 4 slices) bread loaf together to make snake head. Cut bell pepper into 2-inch-long tongue shape. Make very small horizontal slice in heel of bread, being careful not to cut all the way through. Place "tongue" into slice. Cut black olive in half lengthwise; attach with peanut butter to snake head for eyes. Cut 2 small pieces from green olive; attach with peanut butter for nostrils. Set snake head aside.

2. Combine remaining peanut butter, jelly and marshmallow creme in small bowl until smooth. Spread on half of bread slices; top with remaining bread slices.

3. Place snake head on large serving tray. Arrange sandwiches in wavy pattern to resemble slithering snake. Serve immediately.

Makes about 8 small sandwiches

Tacos Olé

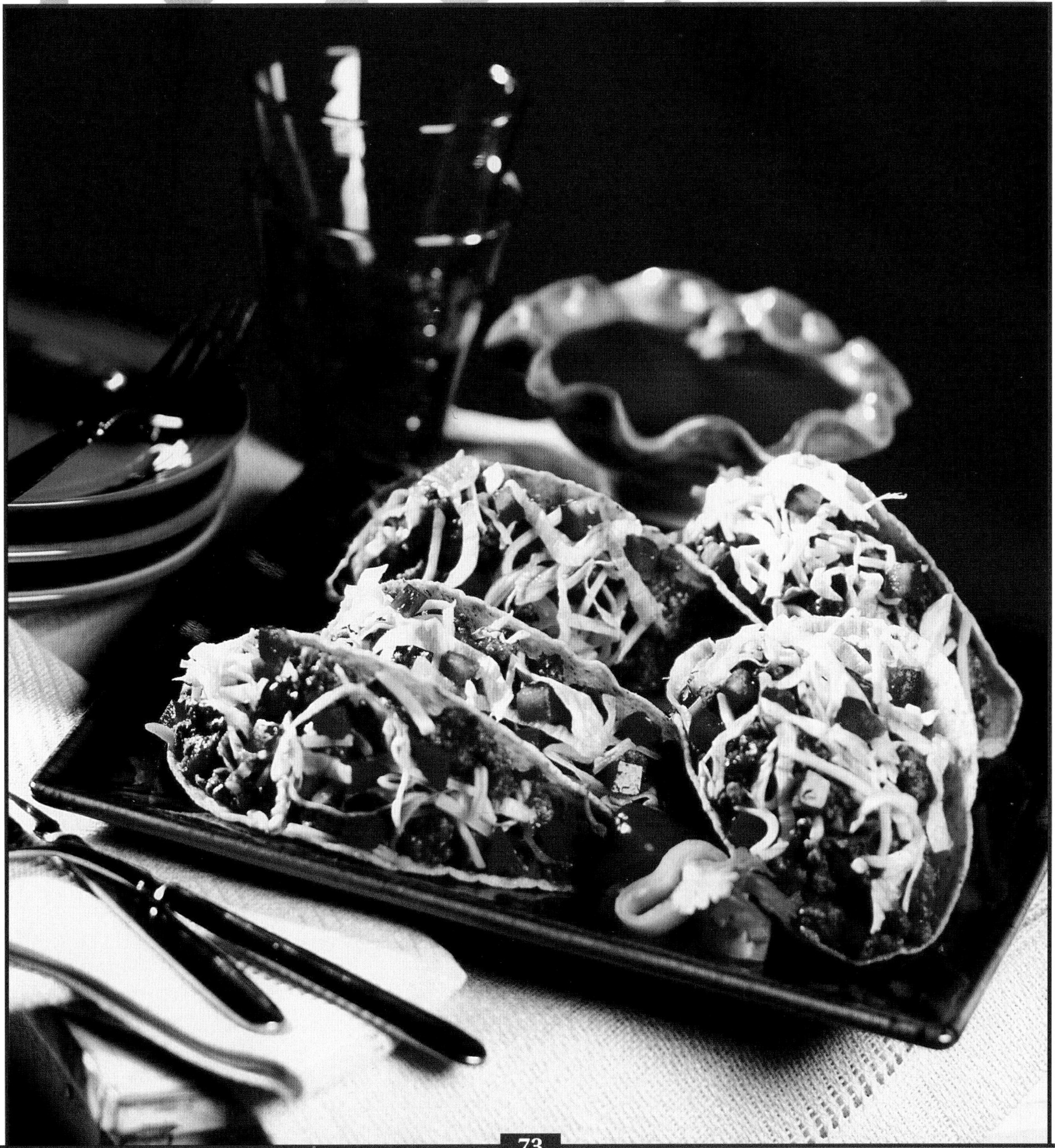

Kids' Wrap

4 teaspoons Dijon honey mustard

2 (8-inch) fat-free flour tortillas

2 slices reduced-fat American cheese, cut in half

4 ounces thinly sliced fat-free oven-roasted turkey breast

½ cup shredded carrot (about 1 medium)

3 romaine lettuce leaves, washed and torn into bite-size pieces

1. Spread 2 teaspoons mustard evenly over one tortilla.

2. Top with 2 cheese halves, half of turkey, half of carrots and half of lettuce.

3. Roll up tortilla and cut in half. Repeat with remaining ingredients.   *Makes 2 servings*

Peanut Butter and Fruit Pita Pockets

1 large crisp apple, peeled, cored and finely diced

1 medium Bartlett pear, peeled, cored and finely diced

1½ teaspoons raisins

2 teaspoons orange juice

3 tablespoons super chunk peanut butter

4 large lettuce leaves or 8 large spinach leaves

2 whole wheat pitas, about 2 ounces each

1. Combine diced apples, pears and raisins with orange juice and hold for 5 minutes. Add peanut butter and mix well.

2. Wash and dry lettuce or spinach leaves on absorbent paper towels. Tear lettuce into pita size pieces.

3. Warm pita in toaster on lowest color setting. Cut pita in half, and carefully open each half to make a pocket.

4. Line each pocket with lettuce or spinach leaves and spoon in equal portions of fruit and peanut butter mixture. Serve and enjoy.
     Makes 4 snack portions or 2 meal portions

Favorite recipe from **Chilean Fresh Fruit Association**

Ham Tortillas with Picante Sauce

2 tablespoons mayonnaise or salad dressing

1 tablespoon picante sauce

2 (8-inch) flour tortillas, warmed

4 thin slices CURE 81® ham

Shredded lettuce

Chopped tomato

In small bowl, combine mayonnaise and picante sauce. Spread tortillas with mayonnaise mixture. Top each tortilla with two ham slices, lettuce and tomato. Roll up. Serve with additional picante sauce, if desired.
     Makes 2 servings

Sloppy Joe's Bun Buggy

4 hot dog buns (not split)

16 thin slices cucumber or zucchini

24 thin strips julienned carrots, 1 inch long

4 ripe olives, halved crosswise

   Nonstick cooking spray

1 (10-ounce) package extra-lean ground turkey

1¼ cups pasta sauce

½ cup chopped broccoli stems

2 teaspoons mustard

½ teaspoon Worcestershire sauce

   Dash salt

   Dash black pepper

4 small pretzel twists

1. Hollow out buns. Use toothpick to make four holes in sides of each bun to attach "wheels." Make hole in center of each cucumber slice; push carrot strip through hole. Press "wheels" into holes in buns.

2. Use toothpick to make two holes in one end of each bun to attach "headlights." Use carrot strips to attach olives to buns, making "headlights."

3. Spray large nonstick skillet with cooking spray. Cook turkey in skillet over medium heat until no longer pink. Stir in pasta sauce, broccoli stems, mustard, Worcestershire, salt and pepper; heat through.

4. Spoon turkey mixture into buns. Press pretzel twist into turkey mixture, making "windshield" on each buggy.

Makes 4 servings

Cartoona Sandwiches

½ cup low fat mayonnaise

½ cup plain low fat yogurt

1½ teaspoons curry powder (optional)

1 cup SUN-MAID® Raisins or Fruit Bits

½ cup diced celery, or red or green bell pepper

1 green onion thinly sliced

1 large can (12 ounces) tuna packed in water, or substitute 1¼ cups chopped cooked chicken (two small chicken breasts)

6 sandwich rolls, round or oblong shaped

1. **MAKE FILLING:** Mix in a medium bowl, the mayonnaise, yogurt, curry powder, if desired, Sun-Maid® Raisins or Fruit Bits, celery or bell pepper, and green onion. Stir in tuna or chicken.

2. **MAKE "CAR":** Cut* a ½-inch slice off the top of a roll. With fingers or a fork, scoop out bread from center of roll.

3. **ATTACH** Sun-Maid® Apricots, carrot slices or other round ingredient to a toothpick to make car "wheels." Insert wheels into bottom edge of roll. Add apple slices for "fenders," if desired.

4. **MAKE** "headlights" using toothpicks to attach raisins on one end of the roll. Cut "doors" in sides of roll, if desired.

5. **FILL** roll with about ½ cup tuna or chicken salad. Place roll top on top of "car." Repeat with remaining rolls. *Makes 6 sandwiches*

*Adult Supervision Suggested

Note: Remove all toothpicks before eating.

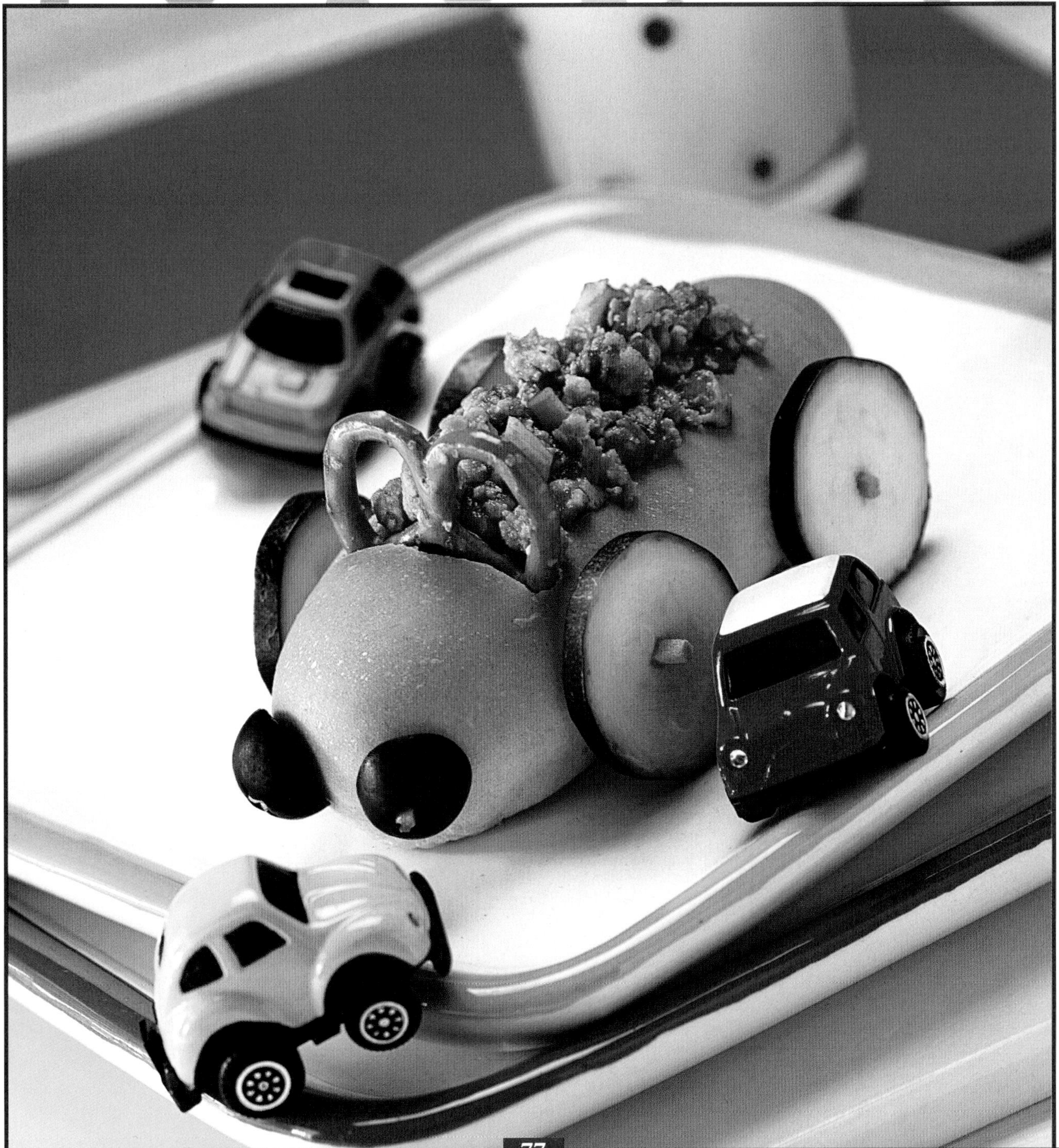

Lumberjacks' Fingers

8 small sandwich rolls
4 frankfurters
   Ketchup
1 radish

1. Use the handle of a wooden spoon to push a 2-inch long hole into the end of each sandwich roll. Don't push all the way through the roll.

2. Slice each frankfurter in half, then cut a notch in the uncut end for a "nail bed." Cook frankfurters according to package directions.

3. Spoon a little ketchup into the hole of each roll. Push a piece of frankfurter into each hole, with the notched end sticking out.

4. Cut 8 thin slices of radish and trim into wedges. Place a radish wedge on the notched end of each frankfurter to make "fingernails." Serve with additional ketchup for dipping.

Makes 4 servings

Chunky Joes

   Nonstick cooking spray
1 pound 95% lean ground beef
1½ cups finely chopped green bell pepper
1 can (14½ ounces) stewed tomatoes
¼ cup water
2 tablespoons tomato paste
1 tablespoon chili powder
1 tablespoon Worcestershire sauce
1 packet sugar substitute
1 teaspoon ground cumin, divided
6 hamburger buns, warmed

1. Lightly coat 12-inch skillet with cooking spray. Heat over high heat until hot. Add beef; cook and stir 3 minutes or until no longer pink. Drain on paper towels; set aside. Wipe out skillet with paper towel.

2. Coat skillet with cooking spray; heat over medium-high heat until hot. Add beef and bell pepper; cook and stir 4 minutes or until bell pepper is just tender. Add tomatoes, water, tomato paste, chili powder, Worcestershire, sugar substitute and ½ teaspoon cumin. Bring to a boil. Reduce heat and simmer, covered, 20 minutes or until thickened.

3. Remove from heat and stir in remaining ½ teaspoon cumin. For thicker consistency, cook 5 minutes longer, uncovered, stirring frequently.

4. Spoon ½ cup mixture onto each bun.

Makes 6 servings

Apricot Chicken Sandwiches

6 ounces chicken tenders, poached and chopped

2 tablespoons fruit-only apricot spread

2 tablespoons chopped fresh apricots (pits removed)

4 slices whole wheat bread

4 lettuce leaves

1. Combine chicken, apricot spread and chopped fruit; mix well.

2. Divide chicken mixture evenly among bread slices. Top bread with lettuce leaves and slice in half, folding over to make a half-sandwich. Slice each half again to make 2 wedges. Serve immediately. *Makes 8 wedges*

Hero SPAM™ Sandwich

1 (16-ounce) loaf Italian bread

2 tablespoons Italian salad dressing

1 (12-ounce) can SPAM® Classic, thinly sliced

1 tomato, thinly sliced

6 ounces sliced provolone cheese

2 to 3 PELOPONNESE® Roasted Florina Sweet Peppers *or* 1 red bell pepper, cut into thin rings

1 small red onion, thinly sliced

10 PELOPONNESE® pitted Kalamata olives, halved

Lettuce leaves

Cut bread in half lengthwise; remove a portion of soft center. Drizzle dressing over cut sides of bread. Layer SPAM®, tomato, cheese, peppers, onion, olives and lettuce over bottom of loaf. Cover with top half of bread; press down to make a compact sandwich. Wrap in foil. Refrigerate 2 hours. Cut crosswise to serve.
Makes 6 servings

Peanut Butter and Jelly Club Sandwich

3 tablespoons JIF® Creamy Peanut Butter

3 slices bread

2 tablespoons SMUCKER'S® Strawberry Jam

½ banana, sliced

2 strawberries, sliced

1. Spread JIF® peanut butter on 2 slices of bread. Spread SMUCKER'S® Strawberry Jam on the remaining slice of bread.

2. Place sliced banana on top of 1 slice of bread with JIF® peanut butter. Place sliced strawberries on top of other piece of bread with JIF® peanut butter.

3. Put piece of bread with strawberries on top of bread with bananas. Close sandwich with slice of bread with SMUCKER'S® Strawberry Jam facing down. *Makes 1 serving*

Hot Dog Burritos

1 can (16 ounces) pork and beans

⅓ cup ketchup

2 tablespoons brown sugar

2 tablespoons *French's*® Classic Yellow® Mustard

8 frankfurters, cooked

8 (8-inch) flour tortillas, heated

1. Combine beans, ketchup, brown sugar and mustard in medium saucepan. Bring to boil over medium-high heat. Reduce heat to low and simmer 2 minutes.

2. Arrange frankfurters in heated tortillas and top with bean mixture. Roll up jelly-roll style.

Makes 8 servings

Tip: Try topping dogs with *French's*® French Fried Onions before rolling up!

Prep Time: 5 minutes
Cook Time: 8 minutes

Barbecue Flying Saucers

½ teaspoon black pepper*

1 (10-ounce) pork tenderloin*

¼ cup barbecue sauce

½ teaspoon mustard

1 (7½-ounce) package refrigerated buttermilk biscuits (10 biscuits)

1 egg yolk (optional)

1 teaspoon water (optional)

3 to 4 drops food coloring (optional)

*Substitute 10 ounces lean deli roasted pork for pork tenderloin and pepper, if desired.

1. Preheat oven to 425°F. Rub pepper on outside of pork tenderloin. Place pork in shallow roasting pan. Roast 15 to 25 minutes or until meat thermometer inserted into thickest part of meat registers 160°F. Remove from oven; let stand 5 minutes. Shred pork.

2. *Reduce oven temperature to 400°F.* Stir together barbecue sauce and mustard. Toss with shredded pork.

3. Roll each biscuit on lightly floured surface into 4-inch circle. Place one fifth of pork mixture on each of five circles. Moisten edges. Top with remaining biscuit circles. Crimp edges to seal.

4. Stir together egg yolk, water and food coloring to make egg-wash paint, if desired. Using clean paintbrush, paint desired designs on biscuit "flying saucers." Place on baking sheet. Bake 11 to 13 minutes or until golden.

Makes 5 servings

Sandwiches

Hot Dog Burrito

Sub on the Run

2 hard rolls (2 ounces each), split into halves

4 tomato slices

14 turkey pepperoni slices

2 ounces fat-free oven-roasted turkey breast

¼ cup (1 ounce) shredded part-skim mozzarella or reduced-fat sharp Cheddar cheese

1 cup packaged coleslaw mix or shredded lettuce

¼ medium green bell pepper, thinly sliced (optional)

2 tablespoons prepared fat-free Italian salad dressing

1. Top both bottom halves of rolls with 2 tomato slices, 7 pepperoni slices, half of turkey, 2 tablespoons cheese, ½ cup coleslaw mix and half of bell pepper slices, if desired.

2. Drizzle with salad dressing. Top with roll tops. Cut into halves, if desired.

Makes 2 servings

Baked Grilled Cheese Sandwiches

3 tablespoons butter, softened

8 slices bread

4 slices Monterey Jack cheese

4 slices sharp Cheddar cheese

1. Preheat oven to 350°F. Spread butter on one side of each bread slice. Place bread buttered side down on ungreased cookie sheet.

2. Layer 1 slice Monterey Jack and 1 slice Cheddar cheese on four bread slices.

3. Bake 10 to 12 minutes or until cheese is melted. Close sandwiches, placing one plain bread slice buttered side up on cheese.

Makes 4 servings

Sub on the Run

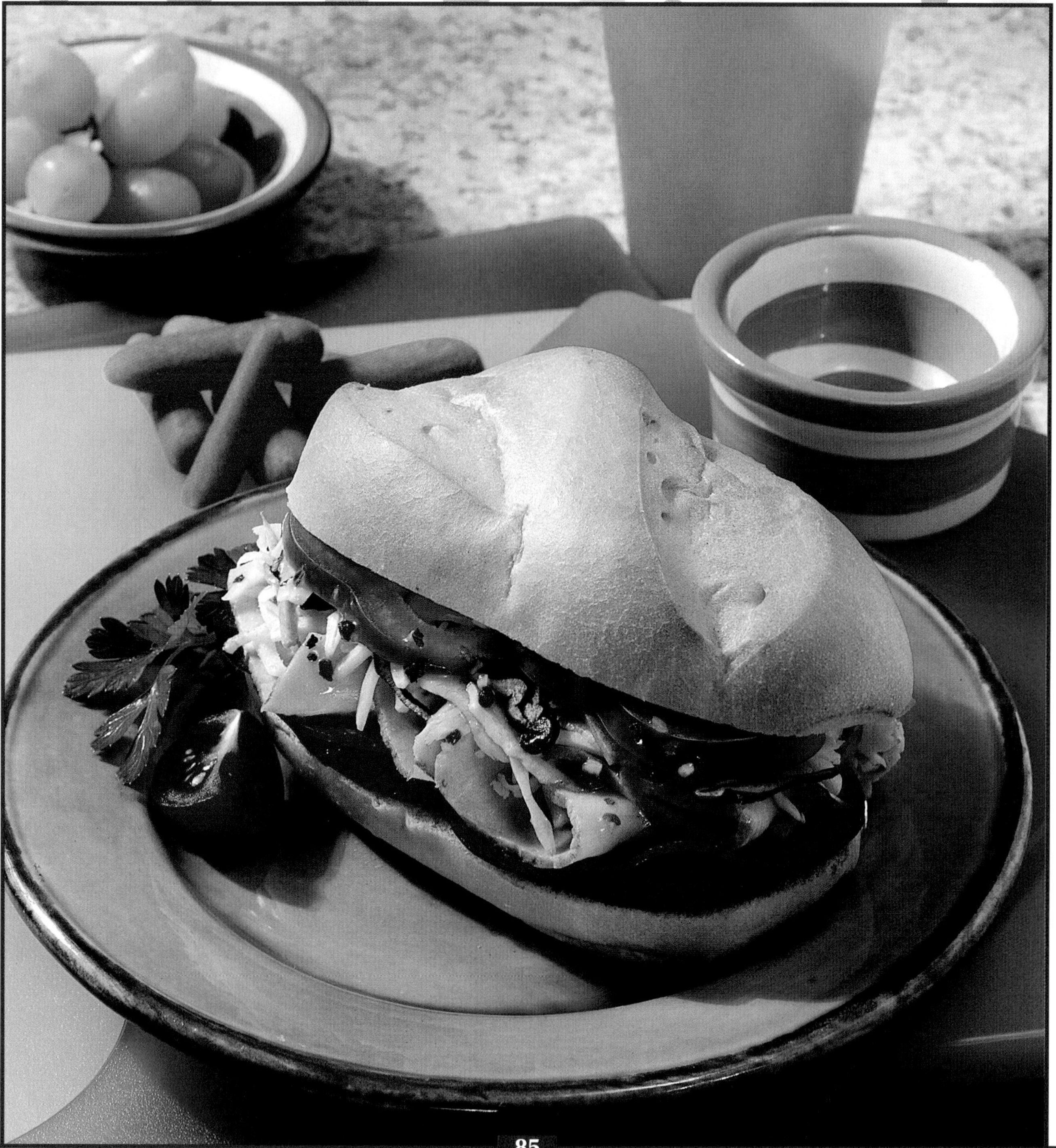

Monster Finger Sandwiches

1 can (11 ounces) refrigerated breadstick dough (12 breadsticks)

Mustard

12 slices deli ham, cut into ½-inch strips

4 slices Monterey Jack cheese, cut into ½-inch strips

1 egg yolk, lightly beaten

Assorted food colorings

1. Preheat oven to 350°F. Place 6 breadsticks on ungreased baking sheets. Spread with mustard as desired. Divide ham strips evenly among breadsticks, placing over mustard. Repeat with cheese. Top with remaining 6 breadsticks. Gently stretch top dough over filling; press dough together to seal.

2. Score knuckle and nail lines into each sandwich using sharp knife. Do not cut completely through dough. Tint egg yolk with food coloring as desired. Paint "fingernail" with egg yolk mixture.

3. Bake on lower oven rack 12 to 13 minutes or just until light golden. Let cool slightly. Serve warm or cool completely.   *Makes 6 servings*

Philadelphia Cheesesteak Sandwich

1 large Spanish or sweet onion, sliced

1 green bell pepper, cut into thin strips (optional)

1 tablespoon butter

4 (6-inch) French rolls

1 pound rare roast beef slices

4 slices SARGENTO® Deli Style Sliced Mozzarella Cheese, cut into halves

1. In medium skillet, cook onion and pepper in butter. Split rolls almost all the way through. Layer meat and onion mixture in rolls; top each with cheese.

2. Place on baking sheet. Broil 5 inches from heat source, 2 to 3 minutes or until cheese is melted.   *Makes 4 sandwiches*

Prep Time: 12 minutes
Cook Time: 3 minutes

Super Spread Sandwich Stars

1 **Red or Golden Delicious apple, peeled, cored and coarsely chopped**

1 **cup roasted peanuts**

⅓ **cup honey**

1 **tablespoon lemon juice**

1 **teaspoon ground cinnamon**

Sliced sandwich bread

For Super Spread, place chopped apple, peanuts, honey, lemon juice and cinnamon in food processor or blender. Pulse food processor several times until ingredients start to blend, occasionally scraping down the sides with rubber spatula. Process 1 to 2 minutes until mixture is smooth and spreadable.

For Sandwich Stars, use butter knife to spread about 1 tablespoon Super Spread on 2 slices of bread. Stack them together, spread side up. Top with third slice bread. Place cookie cutter on top of sandwich; press down firmly and evenly. Leaving cookie cutter in place, remove excess trimmings with your fingers or a butter knife. Remove cookie cutter.

Makes 1¼ cups spread (about 10 servings)

Favorite recipe from **Texas Peanut Producers Board**

Chicken Dogs on a Stick

1 **tube (8 ounces) refrigerated crescent dinner rolls (8 rolls)**

1 **pound boneless skinless chicken breast halves**

3 **tablespoons CRISCO® Oil***

¾ **cup shredded Romano cheese**

1 **package (3 ounces) cream cheese, softened**

¼ **cup chopped onion**

3 **tablespoons grated Parmesan cheese**

¼ **teaspoon Italian seasoning**

¼ **teaspoon pepper**

8 **frozen treat sticks**

Use your favorite Crisco Oil product.

Heat oven to 375°F.

Separate roll dough into triangles. Stretch each triangle into rectangle about 4 inches long.

Rinse chicken; pat dry. Cut into small cubes. Heat oil in medium skillet on high heat. Add chicken. Stir-fry about 3 minutes or until no longer pink in center. Drain. Cool.

Combine Romano cheese, cream cheese, onion, Parmesan cheese, Italian seasoning, pepper and chicken in medium bowl. Mix well. Spoon about ⅓ cup filling onto each dough rectangle. Wrap around wooden stick so that one end of stick can be used as "handle." Press and pinch dough ends to seal.

Bake for 15 to 20 minutes or until browned. Cool on rack 5 to 10 minutes before serving.

Makes 8 servings

Monster Sandwiches

8 assorted sandwich rolls

Butter

16 to 24 slices assorted cold cuts (salami, turkey, ham and/or bologna)

6 to 8 slices assorted cheeses (American, Swiss and/or Muenster)

1 firm tomato, sliced

1 cucumber, thinly sliced

Assorted lettuce leaves (Romaine, curly and/or red leaf)

Cocktail onions, green and black olives, cherry tomatoes, pickled gherkins, radishes, baby corn and/or hard-boiled eggs

1. Cut rolls open just below center; spread with butter.

2. Layer meats, cheeses, tomato, cucumber and greens to make monster faces. Roll "tongues" from ham slices or make "lips" with tomato slices.

3. Use toothpicks to affix remaining ingredients for eyes, ears, fins, horns and hair as desired.   *Makes 8 sandwiches*

Note: Remember to remove toothpicks before eating.

Sloppy Joes

1 pound ground beef or turkey

1 can (10¾ ounces) condensed tomato soup

2 tablespoons *French's®* Worcestershire Sauce

4 large rolls, split

Garnish: shredded Cheddar cheese, sliced green onions, chopped tomatoes

1. Cook beef in large skillet until browned; drain. Add soup, *¼ cup water* and Worcestershire. Heat to boiling. Simmer over low heat 5 minutes, stirring often.

2. Serve in rolls. Top with cheese, onions and tomatoes.   *Makes 4 servings*

Prep Time: 5 minutes
Cook Time: 10 minutes

Campfire Hot Dogs

½ pound ground beef

2 cups RAGÚ® Old World Style® Pasta Sauce

1 can (10¾ to 16 ounces) baked beans

8 frankfurters, cooked

8 frankfurter rolls

1. In 12-inch skillet, brown ground beef over medium-high heat; drain.

2. Stir in Ragú Pasta Sauce and beans. Bring to a boil over high heat. Reduce heat to low and simmer, stirring occasionally, 5 minutes.

3. To serve, arrange frankfurters in rolls and top with sauce mixture. Garnish, if desired, with Cheddar cheese.   *Makes 8 servings*

Tip: For Chili Campfire Hot Dogs, simply stir 2 to 3 teaspoons chili powder into sauce mixture.

Prep Time: 5 minutes
Cook Time: 10 minutes

Sloppy Dogs

1 can (15 ounces) pinto or kidney beans, drained

1 can (14½ ounces) DEL MONTE® Diced Tomatoes Zesty Chili Style

2 fully cooked hot dogs, sliced crosswise

1 teaspoon prepared mustard

4 hamburger buns, split

½ cup shredded Cheddar cheese

Microwave Directions

1. Combine all ingredients, except buns and cheese in 2-quart microwavable dish. Cover and microwave on HIGH 6 to 8 minutes or until heated through.

2. Place buns on paper towel; microwave on HIGH 30 seconds to 1 minute. Place buns on 4 dishes, cut side up.

3. Spoon chili over buns. Top with cheese. Serve immediately.   *Makes 4 servings*

Prep Time: 5 minutes
Cook Time: 9 minutes

Funny Face Sandwich Melts

2 super-size English muffins, split and
    toasted

8 teaspoons *French's*® Sweet & Tangy
    Honey Mustard

1 can (8 ounces) crushed pineapple,
    drained

8 ounces sliced smoked ham

4 slices Swiss cheese or white American
    cheese

1. Place English muffins, cut side up, on
baking sheet. Spread each with *2 teaspoons*
mustard. Arrange one-fourth of the pineapple,
ham and cheese on top, dividing evenly.

2. Broil until cheese melts, about 1 minute.
Decorate with mustard and assorted
vegetables to create your own funny face.
Makes 4 servings

Tip: This sandwich is also easy to prepare in
the toaster oven.

Prep Time: 10 minutes
Cook Time: 1 minute

Corny Sloppy Joes

1 pound lean ground beef or ground
    turkey

1 small onion, chopped

1 can (15½ ounces) sloppy joe sauce

1 box (10 ounces) BIRDS EYE® frozen
    Sweet Corn

6 hamburger buns

• In large skillet, cook beef and onion over high
heat until beef is well browned.

• Stir in sloppy joe sauce and corn; reduce heat
to low and simmer 5 minutes or until heated
through.

• Serve mixture in hamburger buns.
Makes 6 servings

Serving Suggestion: Sprinkle with shredded
Cheddar cheese.

Prep Time: 5 minutes
Cook Time: 15 minutes

Sassy Southwestern Veggie Wraps

½ cup diced zucchini

½ cup diced red or yellow bell pepper

½ cup frozen corn, thawed and drained

1 jalapeño pepper,* seeded and chopped

¾ cup shredded reduced-fat Mexican cheese blend

3 tablespoons prepared salsa or picante sauce

2 (8-inch) fat-free flour tortillas

Jalapeño peppers can sting and irritate the skin; wear rubber gloves when handling peppers and do not touch eyes. Wash hands after handling.

1. Combine zucchini, bell pepper, corn and jalapeño pepper in small bowl. Stir in cheese and salsa; mix well.

2. Soften tortillas according to package directions. Spoon vegetable mixture down center of tortillas, distributing evenly; roll up burrito-style. Serve wraps cold or warm.** Garnish as desired.   *Makes 2 servings*

**To warm each wrap, cover loosely with plastic wrap and microwave at HIGH 40 to 45 seconds or until cheese is melted.*

Crunchy Turkey Pita Pockets

1 cup diced cooked turkey or chicken breast or reduced-sodium deli turkey breast

½ cup packaged cole slaw mix

½ cup dried cranberries

¼ cup shredded carrots

2 tablespoons mayonnaise

1 tablespoon honey mustard

2 whole wheat pita breads

1. Combine turkey, cole slaw mix, cranberries, carrots, mayonnaise and mustard in small bowl; mix well.

2. Cut pita breads in half; fill with turkey mixture.   *Makes 2 servings*

Sandwiches

Sassy Southwestern Veggie Wrap

Bologna "Happy Faces"

4 slices whole wheat or rye bread

1 cup prepared oil and vinegar based
    coleslaw

8 ounces HEBREW NATIONAL® Sliced
    Lean Beef Bologna or Lean Beef
    Salami

4 large pimiento-stuffed green olives

    HEBREW NATIONAL® Deli Mustard

For each sandwich, spread 1 bread slice with
3 tablespoons coleslaw; top with 5 slices
bologna. Cut olives in half crosswise; place
over bologna for "eyes." Draw smiley "mouth"
with mustard. Drop 1 tablespoon coleslaw at
top of face for "hair."

Makes 4 open-faced sandwiches

Tacklin' Turkey Joes

1 pound lean ground turkey

1½ teaspoons chili powder

12 ounces HEINZ® Homestyle Zesty Onion
    Gravy

1 cup HEINZ® Tomato Ketchup

⅓ cup HEINZ® Sweet Relish

6 sandwich buns

In large skillet, brown turkey, drain fat. Stir in
chili powder then add gravy, ketchup and
relish. Simmer uncovered for 5 minutes. Serve
in buns. *Makes 6 servings*

Bologna "Happy Faces"

Operation Thirst

Peanut Butter & Jelly Shakes

1½ cups vanilla ice cream

¼ cup milk

2 tablespoons creamy peanut butter

6 peanut butter sandwich cookies, coarsely chopped

¼ cup strawberry preserves

1. Place ice cream, milk and peanut butter in blender. Blend at medium speed 1 to 2 minutes or until smooth and well blended. Add chopped cookies; blend 10 seconds at low speed. Pour into 2 serving glasses.

2. Place preserves and 1 to 2 teaspoons water in small bowl; stir until smooth. Stir 2 tablespoons preserve mixture into each glass. Serve immediately.   *Makes 2 servings*

Variation: For a change of pace, prepare these shakes using different flavors of preserves.

Prep Time: 10 minutes

Fruit 'n Juice Breakfast Shake

1 extra-ripe, medium DOLE® Banana
¾ cup DOLE® Pineapple Juice
½ cup lowfat vanilla yogurt
½ cup blueberries

Combine all ingredients in blender. Process until smooth. *Makes 2 servings*

Cookie Milk Shakes

1 pint vanilla ice cream
4 chocolate sandwich cookies or chocolate-covered graham crackers

Scoop ice cream into blender fitted with metal blade. Crush cookies in resealable plastic food storage bag with rolling pin or food processor. Place cookies in blender. Process until well combined. Pour into 2 glasses. Serve immediately. *Makes 2 milk shakes*

Maraschino Cherry Shake

1 (10-ounce) jar maraschino cherries
3 tablespoons maraschino cherry juice
3 cups vanilla ice cream
Whipped topping
Whole maraschino cherries, for garnish

1. Put a colander or strainer in a bowl. Pour cherries into the strainer. Measure out 3 tablespoons of juice and put it in a small container. You will use these 3 tablespoons of juice to prepare this recipe. You can either discard the remaining juice or save it for another use.

2. Put cherries from the strainer on a cutting board. With a sharp knife, carefully cut cherries into small pieces. Have an adult show you how to use the knife.

3. Put chopped cherries, 3 tablespoons juice and ice cream in the container of an electric blender or food processor; cover blender. Process or blend until smooth. Do not put a spoon or spatula in the blender while it is running and keep your hands clear of the working parts.

4. Pour into 2 (12-ounce) glasses. Top with whipped topping; garnish with whole maraschino cherries. *Makes 2 (12-ounce) servings*

Favorite recipe from **Cherry Marketing Institute**

Fruit 'n Juice Breakfast Shake

Sinister Slushies

4 bottles brightly colored sport drinks

4 to 8 ice cube trays

1. Pour sport drinks into separate ice cube trays and freeze overnight.

2. Just before serving, place frozen cubes into large resealable plastic food storage bags one color at a time. Seal bag and smash cubes with rolling pin.

3. Layer different colored ice slush in clear glasses to make wild combinations. Serve immediately with straws or spoons.

Makes 4 to 8 servings

Glowing Punch

1 quart ginger ale

1 cup cranberry juice cocktail concentrate

1 cup mango, orange or peach sherbet or sorbet

Fruit leathers

1. Combine ginger ale and cranberry juice concentrate in serving bowl. Drop sherbet by tablespoonfuls into punch.

2. Using small cookie cutters, cut shapes out of fruit leathers. Sprinkle shapes over sherbet or use to garnish punch glasses. Serve immediately. *Makes 6 servings*

Cherry-Berry Smoothie

1 cup frozen whole unsweetened pitted dark sweet cherries

1 cup frozen whole unsweetened strawberries

1 cup cranberry-cherry juice

In blender, purée frozen pitted dark sweet cherries, frozen strawberries and juice, stirring as needed, until smooth.

Makes 1 (16-ounce) serving

Note: Frozen pitted dark sweet cherries may be replaced with ¾ cup well-drained canned pitted dark sweet cherries and four ice cubes.

Favorite recipe from **Northwest Cherry Growers**

Golden Harvest Punch

4 cups MOTT'S® Apple Juice

4 cups orange juice

3 liters club soda

1 quart orange sherbet

5 pound bag ice cubes (optional)

Combine apple juice, orange juice and club soda in punch bowl. Add scoops of sherbet or ice, if desired. *Makes 25 servings*

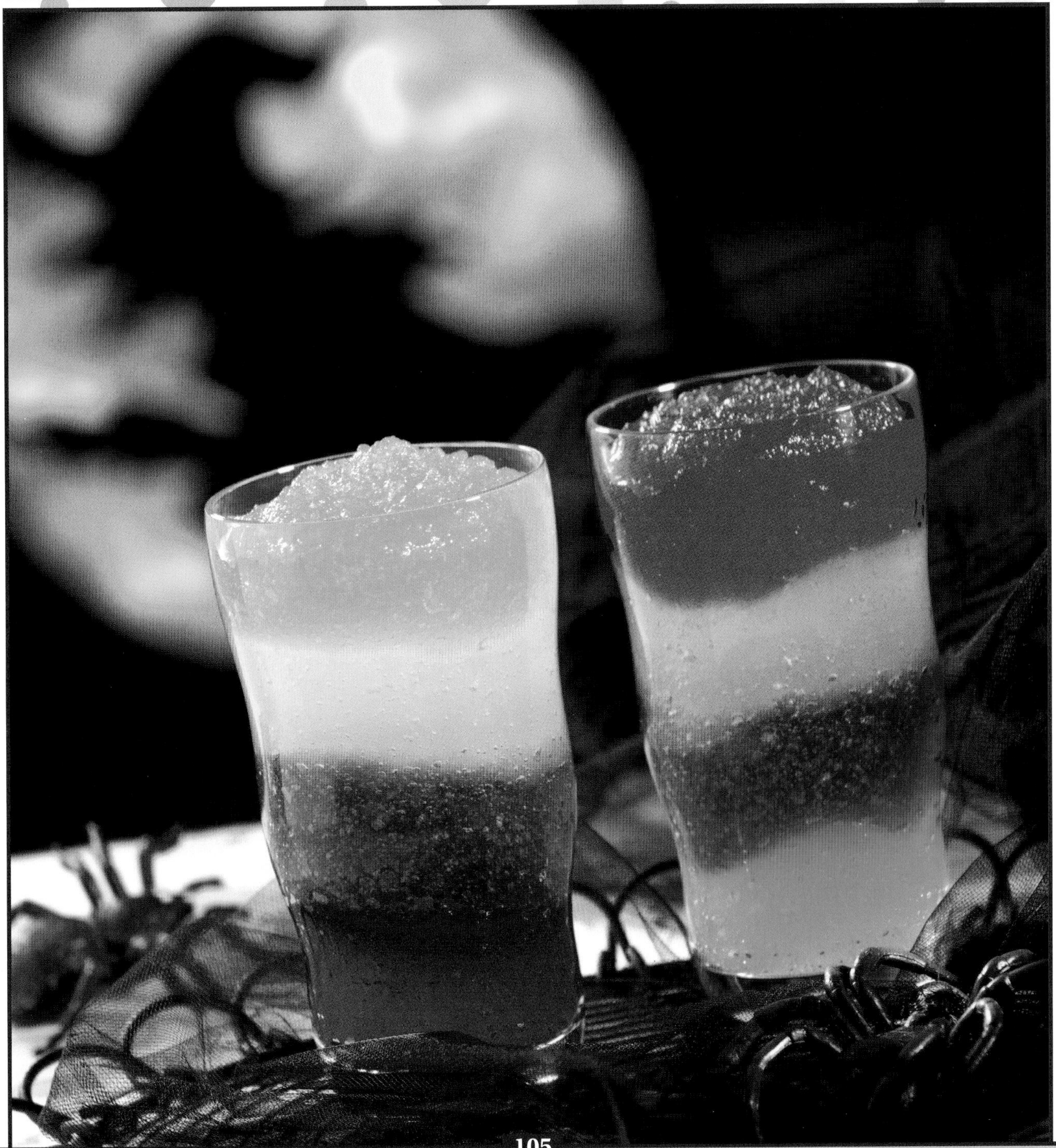

Oregon Hot Apple Cider

8 cups apple cider

½ cup dried cherries

½ cup dried cranberries

3 cinnamon sticks, broken in half

8 whole cloves

1 pear, quartered, cored, sliced

1. Combine cider, cherries, cranberries, cinnamon sticks and cloves in large saucepan. Heat just to a simmer; do not boil.

2. Add pear before serving.

Makes 16 (½-cup) servings

Chocolate Mint Cooler

2 cups cold whole milk or half-and-half

¼ cup chocolate syrup

1 teaspoon peppermint extract

Crushed ice

Aerosol whipped topping

Mint leaves

Combine milk, chocolate syrup and peppermint extract in small pitcher; stir until well blended. Fill 2 glasses with crushed ice. Pour chocolate mint mixture over ice. Top with whipped topping and garnish with mint leaves.

Makes 2 servings

Peanut Butter-Banana Shake

1 ripe banana, cut into chunks

1 cup milk

½ cup vanilla ice cream

2 tablespoons peanut butter

Place all ingredients in blender container. Cover; process until smooth.

Makes about 2 cups

Berry-Banana Breakfast Smoothie

1 carton (8 ounces) berry-flavored yogurt

1 ripe banana, cut into chunks

½ cup milk

Place all ingredients in blender. Cover; blend until smooth.

Makes about 2 cups

Oregon Hot Apple Cider

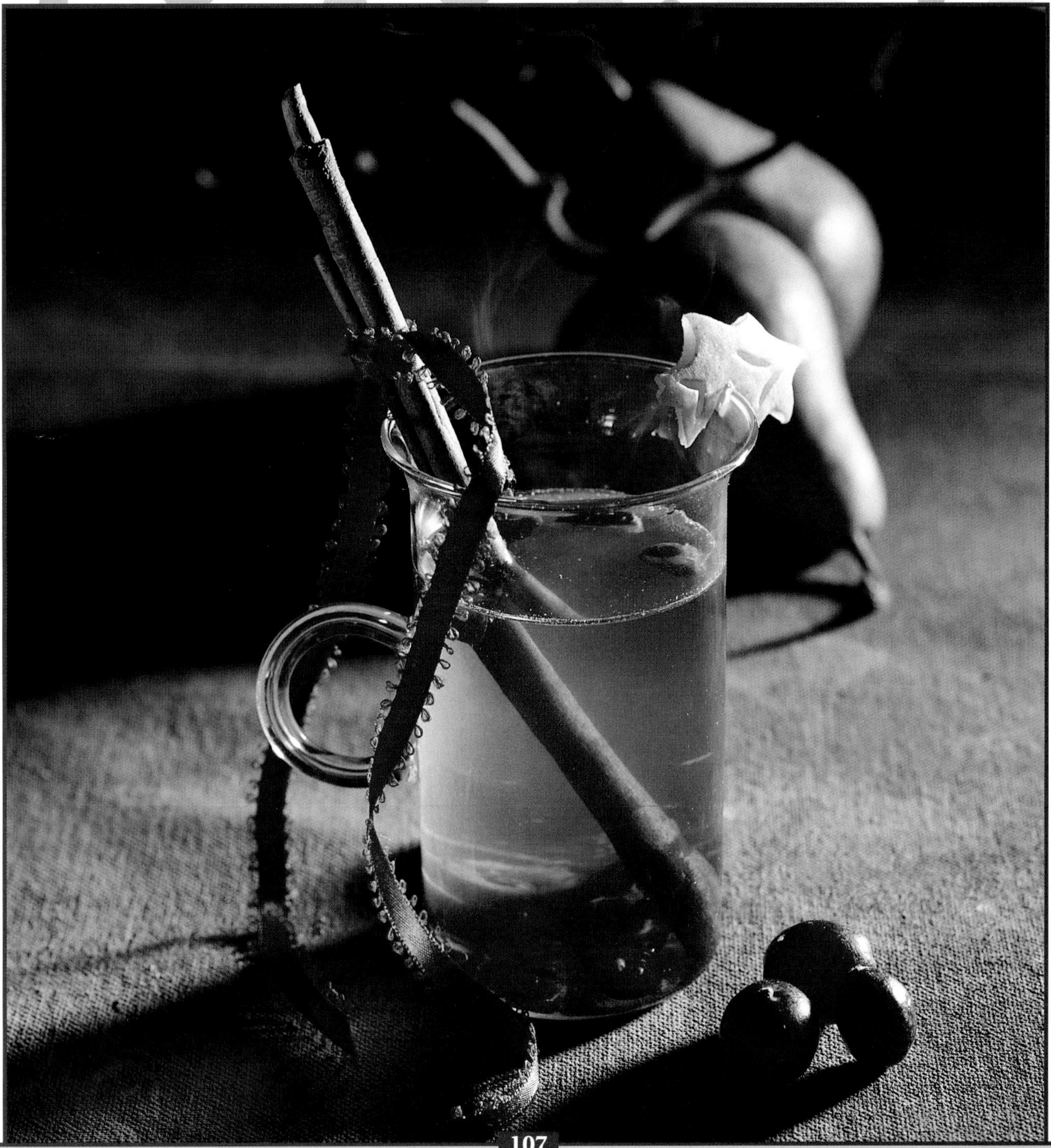

Banana Smoothies & Pops

1 (14-ounce) can EAGLE BRAND®
  Sweetened Condensed Milk (NOT
  evaporated milk)
1 (8-ounce) container vanilla yogurt
2 ripe bananas
½ cup orange juice

1. In blender container, combine all ingredients; blend until smooth. Stop occasionally to scrape down sides.

2. Serve immediately. Store covered in refrigerator.   *Makes 4 cups*

Banana Smoothie Pops: Spoon banana mixture into 8 (5-ounce) paper cups. Freeze 30 minutes. Insert wooden craft sticks into the center of each cup; freeze until firm. Makes 8 pops

Fruit Smoothies: Substitute 1 cup of your favorite fruit and ½ cup any fruit juice for banana and orange juice.

Prep Time: 5 minutes

Spiced Cider Punch (Goblin's Brew)

4 cups water
1 cup packed brown sugar
¾ cup granulated sugar
4 cinnamon sticks
¼ teaspoon whole cloves
4 cups freshly squeezed SUNKIST® orange
  juice
3 cups apple cider
  Juice of 9 SUNKIST® lemons (1½ cups)
  Whole cloves
  Unpeeled SUNKIST® lemon cartwheel
  slices

In large saucepan, combine water, sugars, cinnamon and cloves. Bring to a boil, stirring to dissolve sugars. Reduce heat; simmer 5 minutes. Remove cinnamon and cloves. Add orange juice, cider and lemon juice; heat. Garnish with clove-studded lemon cartwheels.
Makes 13 cups (twenty-six ½-cup servings)

Banana Smoothie & Pops

Dripping Blood Punch

8 thick slices cucumber

4 cups pineapple juice

1 cup orange juice

2 cups ginger ale

  Ice

8 tablespoons grenadine syrup

1. Cut cucumber slices into vampire fangs.

2. Combine pineapple and orange juices in large pitcher. Refrigerate until serving time.

3. Immediately before serving, stir ginger ale into juices. Fill glasses generously with ice and add vampire fangs to rims. Pour punch into ice-filled glasses. Slowly drizzle 1 tablespoon grenadine over top of each serving.

Makes 8 servings

Peanut Butter Chocolate Twist Shake

6 ounces vanilla frozen yogurt or ice cream

4 ounces coconut juice or milk

1 ounce chocolate chips

1 ounce peanut butter

2 curls shaved chocolate

½ ounce crushed roasted peanuts

Whip all ingredients except shaved chocolate and peanuts together in blender until smooth. Garnish with shaved chocolate and crushed roasted peanuts. *Makes 1 serving*

Favorite recipe from **Peanut Advisory Board**

Magic Potion

Creepy Crawler Ice Ring (recipe follows)

1 cup boiling water

2 packages (4-serving size each) lime-flavored gelatin

3 cups cold water

1½ quarts carbonated lemon-lime beverage, chilled

½ cup superfine sugar

Gummy worms (optional)

1. One day ahead, prepare Creepy Crawler Ice Ring.

2. Pour boiling water over gelatin in heatproof punch bowl; stir until gelatin dissolves. Stir in cold water. Add lemon-lime beverage and sugar; stir well (mixture will foam for several minutes).

3. Unmold ice ring by dipping bottom of mold briefly into hot water. Float ice ring in punch. Serve cups of punch garnished with gummy worms, if desired. *Makes about 10 servings*

Creepy Crawler Ice Ring

1 cup gummy worms or other creepy crawler candy

1 quart lemon-lime sport drink

Arrange gummy worms in bottom of 5-cup ring mold; fill mold with sport drink. Freeze until solid, about 8 hours or overnight.

Makes 1 ice ring

Dripping Blood Punch

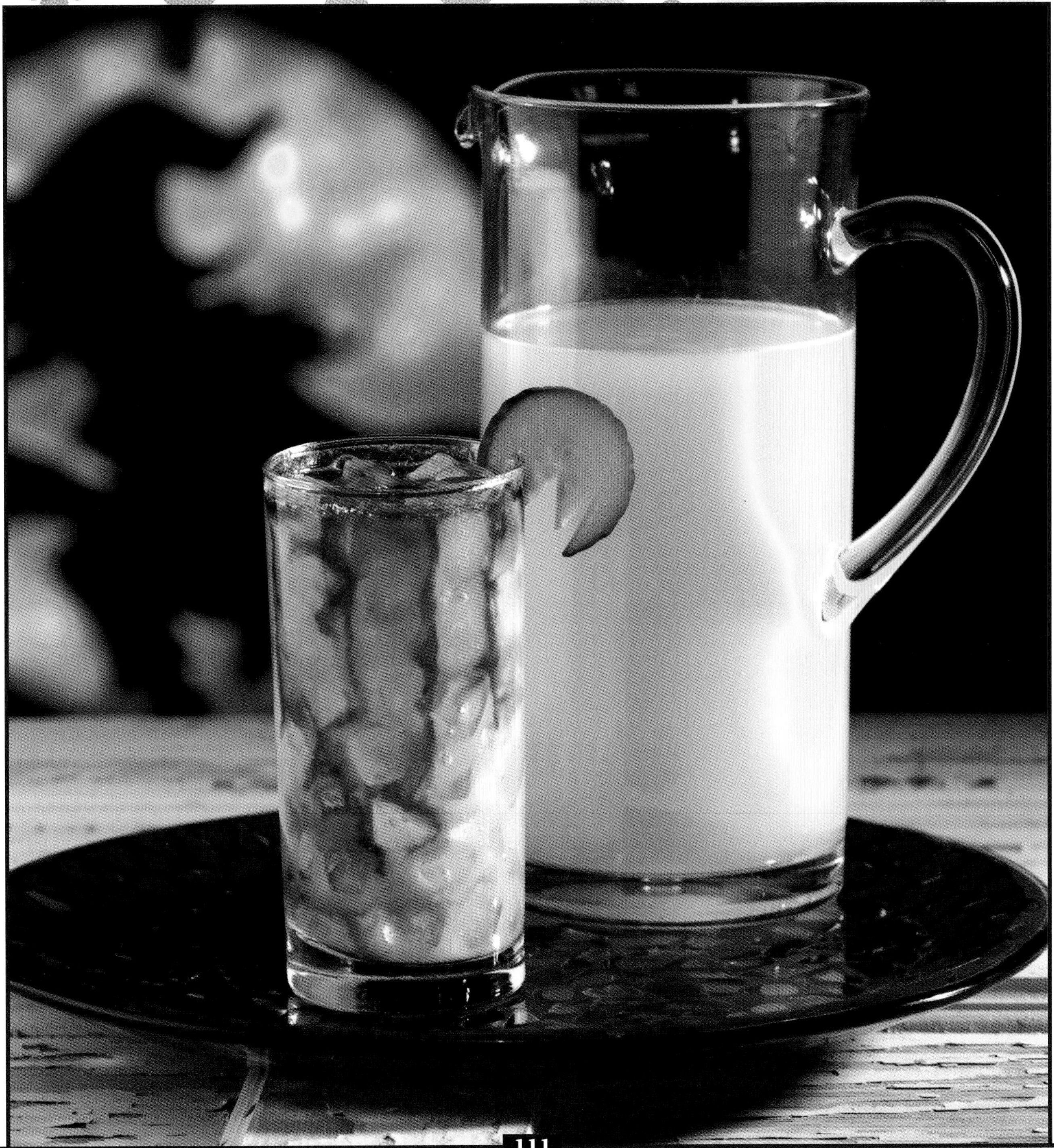

Peanut Butter Shakes

1 cup cold milk
¼ cup JIF® Creamy Peanut Butter
1 cup vanilla ice cream

Place milk and JIF® peanut butter in blender container. Cover and blend until smooth.

Add ice cream; blend until smooth.

Makes 2 servings

Variation: For Banana JIF® Shakes, prepare recipe as directed above, except add a sliced banana to the blender container with the JIF® peanut butter.

Quick Apple Punch

4 cups MOTT'S® Apple Juice
2 cups cranberry juice cocktail
2 tablespoons lemon juice
1 liter ginger ale, chilled
Crushed ice, as needed

In large bowl, combine apple juice, cranberry juice, and lemon juice. Fifteen minutes before serving, add ginger ale and crushed ice. Do not stir.

Makes 15 servings

Trick-or-Treat Punch

Ingredients

Green food coloring
1 envelope (4 ounces) orange-flavored presweetened drink mix
1 can (12 ounces) frozen lemonade concentrate, thawed
1 bottle (2 liters) ginger ale

Supplies

1 new plastic household glove

1. One day ahead, fill pitcher with 3 cups water; tint with green food coloring. Pour into glove; tightly secure top of glove with twist tie. Line baking sheet with paper towels; place glove on prepared baking sheet. Use inverted custard cup to elevate tied end of glove to prevent leaking. Freeze overnight.

2. When ready to serve, combine drink mix, lemonade concentrate and 4 cups water in large bowl; stir until drink mix is dissolved and mixture is well blended. Pour into punch bowl; add ginger ale.

3. Cut glove away from ice; float frozen hand in punch.

Makes 16 (6-ounce) servings and 1 ice hand

Purple Cow Jumped Over the Moon

3 cups vanilla frozen yogurt

1 cup reduced-fat (2%) milk

½ cup thawed frozen grape juice concentrate (undiluted)

1½ teaspoons lemon juice

Place yogurt, milk, grape juice concentrate and lemon juice in food processor or blender container; process until smooth. Serve immediately. *Makes 8 (½-cup) servings*

Razzmatazz Shakes: Place 1 quart vanilla frozen yogurt, 1 cup vanilla yogurt and ¼ cup chocolate syrup in food processor or blender container; process until smooth. Pour ½ of mixture evenly into 12 glasses; top with ½ can (12 ounces) root beer. Fill glasses equally with remaining yogurt mixture; top with remaining root beer. Makes 12 (⅔-cup) servings.

Sunshine Shakes: Place 1 quart vanilla frozen yogurt, 1⅓ cups orange juice, 1 cup fresh or thawed frozen raspberries and 1 teaspoon sugar in food processor or blender container; process until smooth. Pour into 10 glasses; sprinkle with ground nutmeg. Makes 10 (½-cup) servings.

Mint Hot Cocoa with Marshmallows

2 quarts milk

1 cup chocolate-flavored drink mix

1 cup mint-flavored semisweet chocolate chips

16 large marshmallows

1. Combine milk and drink mix in medium saucepan. Stir in chocolate chips. Cook over medium heat, stirring occasionally, until chips are melted and milk is heated through.

2. Place 2 marshmallows in each mug; fill mug with hot cocoa. Serve immediately.
Makes 8 servings

Hot Spiced Cider

2 quarts apple cider

⅔ cup KARO® Light or Dark Corn Syrup

3 cinnamon sticks

½ teaspoon whole cloves

1 lemon, sliced

Cinnamon sticks and lemon slices (optional)

1. In medium saucepan combine cider, corn syrup, cinnamon sticks, cloves and lemon slices.

2. Bring to boil over medium-high heat. Reduce heat; simmer 15 minutes. Remove spices.

3. If desired, garnish each serving with a cinnamon stick and lemon slice.

Makes about 10 servings

Prep Time: 20 minutes

Choco-Berry Cooler

¾ cup cold milk

¼ cup sliced fresh strawberries

2 tablespoons HERSHEY'S Syrup

2 tablespoons plus 2 small scoops vanilla ice cream, divided

Cold ginger ale or club soda

Fresh strawberry

Mint leaves (optional)

1. Place milk, strawberries, chocolate syrup and 2 tablespoons ice cream in blender container. Cover and blend until smooth.

2. Alternate remaining 2 scoops of ice cream and chocolate mixture in tall ice cream soda glass; fill glass with ginger ale. Garnish with a fresh strawberry and mint leaves, if desired. Serve immediately.

Makes one 14-ounce serving

Variations: Before blending, substitute one of the following fruits for fresh strawberries: 3 tablespoons frozen strawberries with syrup, thawed; ½ peeled fresh peach *or* ⅓ cup canned peach slices; 2 slices canned *or* ¼ cup canned crushed pineapple; ¼ cup sweetened fresh raspberries *or* 3 tablespoons frozen raspberries with syrup, thawed.

117

Shamrock Smoothies

1 tablespoon sugar

2 green spearmint candy leaves

2 thin round chocolate mints or chocolate sandwich cookies

1 ripe banana, peeled and cut into chunks

1 cup ice cubes

¾ cup apple juice

¼ cup plain yogurt

½ teaspoon vanilla

¼ teaspoon orange extract

2 or 3 drops green food coloring

1. Place small sheet of waxed paper on work surface; sprinkle with sugar. Place spearmint leaves on waxed paper; top with second sheet of waxed paper. Roll out leaves to ¼-inch thickness. Cut out 2 (1¼×1-inch) shamrock shapes using small knife or scissors. Press 1 shamrock onto each mint; set aside.

2. Place banana, ice cubes, apple juice, yogurt, vanilla, orange extract and food coloring in blender or food processor; blend until smooth and frothy. Pour into glasses. Garnish with mints.

Makes 2 servings (about 8 ounces each)

Chocolate New York Egg Cream

1 square (1 ounce) semisweet chocolate (optional)

¼ cup chocolate syrup

1 cup chilled club soda or carbonated mineral water

Ice

1. Shave chocolate with vegetable peeler, if desired. (Makes about ½ cup.)

2. Pour syrup into 12-ounce glass. Stir in club soda until foamy. Add ice. Garnish with 1 teaspoon chocolate shavings.* Serve immediately.   *Makes 1 serving*

Cover and refrigerate leftover chocolate shavings for another use.

Fat-Free Honey Berry Milkshakes

2½ cups strawberries or assorted berries

1 pint nonfat vanilla frozen yogurt or ice cream

½ cup nonfat milk

¼ cup honey

4 small mint sprigs

Combine all ingredients except mint sprigs in blender or food processor; process about 30 seconds or until smooth. Pour into tall glasses. Garnish with mint sprigs.

Makes 4 cups

Favorite recipe from **National Honey Board**

Witches' Brew

2 cups apple cider

1½ to 2 cups vanilla ice cream

2 tablespoons honey

½ teaspoon ground cinnamon

¼ teaspoon ground nutmeg

Process cider, ice cream, honey, cinnamon and nutmeg in food processor or blender until smooth. Pour into glasses and sprinkle with additional nutmeg. Serve immediately.

Makes 4 (6-ounce) servings

Serving Suggestion: Add a few drops of desired food coloring to ingredients in food processor to make a scary brew.

Lighten Up: To reduce fat, replace vanilla ice cream with reduced-fat or fat-free ice cream or frozen yogurt.

Prep Time: 10 minutes

Bobbing Head Punch

Assorted candies

Assorted fruit slices and pieces

Water

6 cups white grape juice

4 cups ginger ale

2 cups apple juice or 2 additional cups ginger ale

Green food coloring

1. Arrange candy and fruit slices in bottom of 9-inch glass pie plate to create a face. (Remember, the bottom of the face is what will show in the punch bowl.)

2. Add water to cover face; carefully place in freezer. Freeze overnight.

3. Just before serving, combine juices and ginger ale in 4- to 5-quart punch bowl. Tint mixture green. Invert pie plate, placing one hand underneath; run under cold running water to release frozen face. Place ice mold upside down on top of juice mixture; serve.

Makes 20 cups

Operation Thirst

"Moo-vin" Chocolate Milk Shake

1 pint low-fat chocolate ice cream
½ cup fat-free (skim) milk
1 tablespoon chocolate syrup
¼ teaspoon vanilla
⅛ teaspoon decorator sprinkles (optional)

Combine all ingredients except decorator sprinkles in blender container. Cover and blend until smooth. Pour into 2 small glasses. Add decorator sprinkles, if desired. Serve immediately. *Makes 2 servings*

"Moo-vin" Chocolate-Peanut Butter Milk Shake

1 pint low-fat chocolate ice cream
½ cup fat-free (skim) milk
¼ cup creamy peanut butter
¼ teaspoon vanilla
⅛ teaspoon decorator sprinkles (optional)

Combine all ingredients except decorator sprinkles in blender container. Cover and blend until smooth. Pour into 2 small glasses. Add decorator sprinkles, if desired. Serve immediately. *Makes 2 servings*

"Moo-vin" Chocolate-Cherry Milk Shake

1 pint low-fat chocolate ice cream
¾ cup drained canned pitted tart red cherries
¼ cup fat-free (skim) milk
¼ teaspoon vanilla
⅛ teaspoon decorator sprinkles (optional)

Combine all ingredients except decorator sprinkles in blender container. Cover and blend until smooth. Pour into 2 small glasses. Add decorator sprinkles, if desired. Serve immediately. *Makes 2 servings*

"Moo-vin" Strawberry Milk Shake

1 pint low-fat vanilla ice cream
1 cup thawed frozen unsweetened strawberries
¼ cup fat-free (skim) milk
¼ teaspoon vanilla

Combine all ingredients in blender container. Cover and blend until smooth. Pour into 2 small glasses. Serve immediately. *Makes 2 servings*

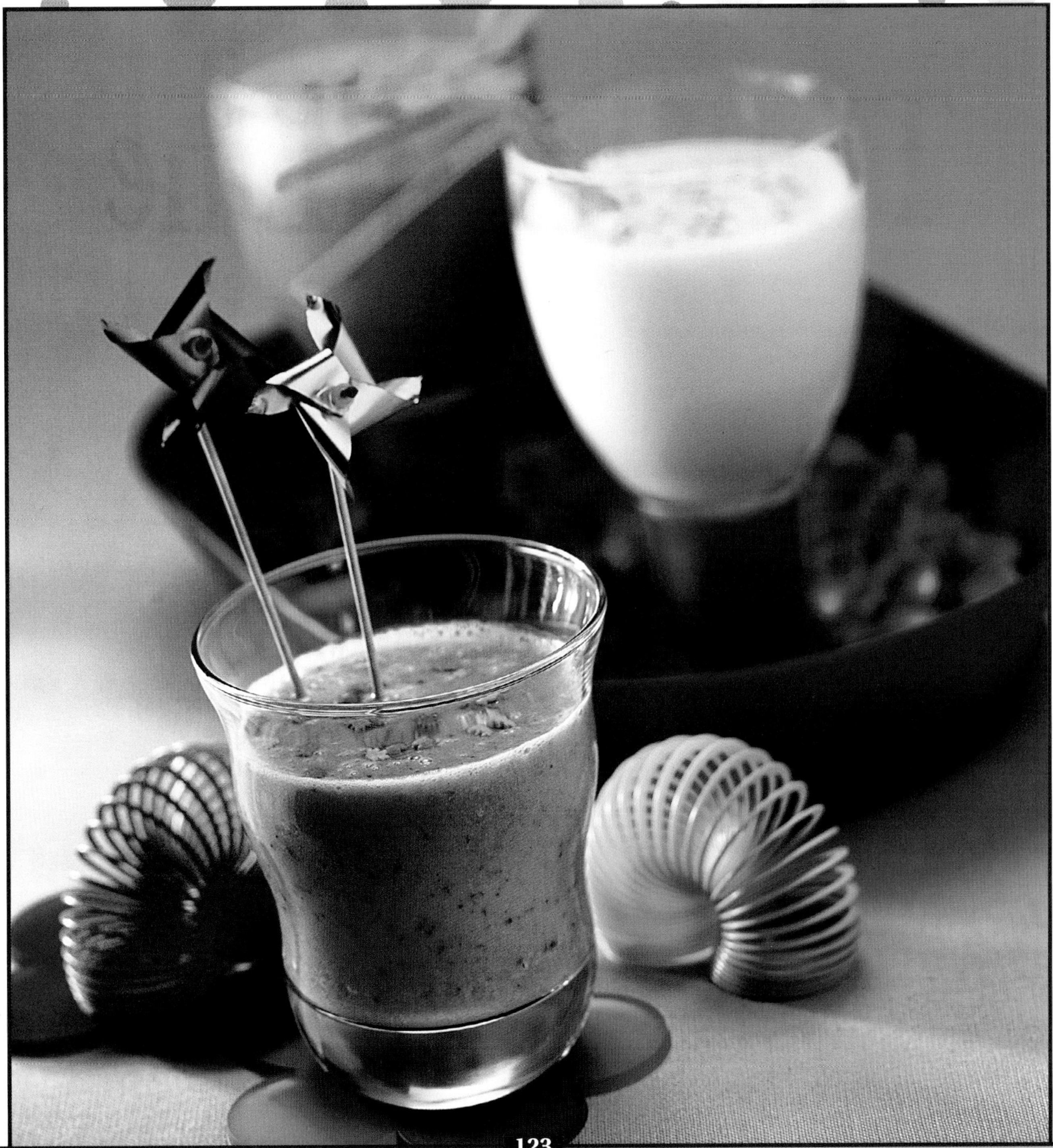

The Finish Line

Cookie Crumb Sundae

1 package (about 18 ounces) chocolate creme-filled sandwich cookies
4 cups milk, divided
1 package (4-serving size) cheesecake-flavored instant pudding mix
1 package (4-serving size) chocolate fudge-flavored instant pudding mix
1 container (8 ounces) frozen whipped topping, thawed
12 to 16 maraschino cherries, drained

1. Place cookies in large resealable plastic food storage bag and crush with rolling pin. Place ¾ of crumbs in bottom of 13×9-inch baking pan.

2. Combine 2 cups milk and cheesecake-flavored pudding mix in large bowl. Prepare according to package directions. Pour pudding evenly over cookie crumbs.

3. Repeat with remaining 2 cups milk and chocolate fudge-flavored pudding mix. Pour evenly over cheesecake pudding.

4. Spread whipped topping over pudding. Sprinkle remaining cookie crumbs over whipped topping. Top with maraschino cherries. Chill 1 hour before serving.
Makes 12 to 14 servings

Variation: This dessert can also be made in individual disposable clear plastic cups. Decorate each with colored sprinkles. They are great for birthdays, holidays and picnics.

Creamy Strawberry-Banana Tart

1 package (16 ounces) frozen unsweetened whole strawberries, thawed

2 tablespoons plus 1½ teaspoons frozen orange juice concentrate, thawed and divided

¼ cup sugar

1 envelope unflavored gelatin

3 egg whites, beaten

1 package (3 ounces) soft ladyfingers, split

4 teaspoons water

½ container (8 ounces) frozen reduced-fat nondairy whipped topping, thawed

1 medium banana, quartered lengthwise and sliced

1 teaspoon multi-colored decorator sprinkles (optional)

1. Place strawberries and 2 tablespoons orange juice concentrate in blender container or food processor bowl. Blend or process until smooth.

2. Combine sugar and gelatin in medium saucepan. Stir in strawberry mixture. Cook, stirring frequently, until boiling.

3. Stir about half of mixture into beaten egg whites. Return all to saucepan. Cook, stirring constantly, over medium heat about 2 minutes or until slightly thickened. (Do not boil.)

4. Pour into bowl. Refrigerate 2 to 2½ hours or until mixture mounds when spooned, stirring occasionally.

5. Cut half of ladyfingers in half crosswise. Place around edge of 9-inch tart pan with removable bottom. Place remaining ladyfingers into bottom of pan, cutting to fit.

6. Stir together remaining 1½ teaspoons orange juice concentrate and water. Drizzle over ladyfingers.

7. Fold thawed dessert topping and banana into strawberry mixture. Spoon into ladyfinger crust. Refrigerate at least 2 hours. Sprinkle with multi-colored sprinkles, if desired. Cut into 10 wedges to serve.   *Makes 10 servings*

Polar Bear Banana Bites

1 medium banana, cut into 6 equal-size pieces

¼ cup creamy peanut butter*

3 tablespoons fat-free (skim) milk

¼ cup miniature-size marshmallows

2 tablespoons unsalted dry-roasted peanuts, chopped (optional)

1 tablespoon chocolate-flavored decorator sprinkles

Soy butter or almond butter can be substituted.

1. Insert toothpick into each banana piece. Place on tray lined with waxed paper.

2. Whisk together peanut butter and milk. Combine marshmallows, peanuts, if desired, and chocolate sprinkles in shallow dish. Dip each banana piece in peanut butter mixture, draining off excess. Roll in marshmallow mixture. Place on tray; let stand until set.
     Makes 3 servings

Wafflewich

2 frozen cinnamon waffles

25 miniature marshmallows

2 tablespoons JIF® Creamy Peanut Butter

½ banana, sliced

¼ cup chocolate chips

1. Toast waffles in the toaster until desired darkness.

2. Heat miniature marshmallows and JIF® in microwave until melted, then mix together.

3. Spread the JIF® peanut butter mixture on waffle.

4. Place banana slices on JIF® peanut butter mixture.

5. Top with chocolate chips.

6. Close sandwich with other waffle.

7. It tastes better warm!

Makes 1 wafflewich

Raisin Apple Puffs

1 small apple

2 tablespoons sugar

1 tablespoon butter

3 eggs

¾ cup milk

½ cup flour

2 tablespoons sugar

Dash of salt

⅓ cup SUN-MAID® Raisins

Powdered sugar

1. **HEAT*** oven to 425°F.

2. **CUT*** unpeeled apple into thin slices. Chop slices into small pieces. There should be about 1 cup of apples.

3. Put apples, sugar and butter in a 10-inch wide ovenproof skillet or deep pie plate. (If skillet has a plastic handle, wrap it in aluminum foil.) Bake for 12 minutes until apples are soft and mixture is bubbly. Hold pan with mitts to remove from oven.

4. While apples are baking, beat eggs, milk, flour, sugar, and salt in a medium bowl, using a whisk or egg beater until frothy and smooth.

5. **STIR*** raisins into apples in hot pan. Pour egg mixture into pan. Hold pan with mitts and place in oven. Bake for 12 to 14 minutes until puffed and golden brown. Check after 8 minutes to watch the puff rise!

6. **SLIDE*** a spatula around edges of pan to loosen puff. Place the top side of a dinner plate over the pan and turn puff out onto the plate. Cut into wedges and serve bottom side up. Sprinkle with powdered sugar. Serve warm.

Makes 4 to 6 servings

*Adult Supervision Suggested

Prep Time: 10 minutes
Bake Time: 25 minutes

Wafflewich

Mud Cups

1 package (18 ounces) refrigerated sugar
    cookie dough
¼ cup unsweetened cocoa powder
3 containers (4 ounces each) chocolate
    pudding
1¼ cups chocolate sandwich cookie crumbs
    (about 15 cookies)
    Gummy worms

1. Preheat oven to 350°F. Grease 18 (2½- or
2¾-inch) muffin pan cups.

2. Remove dough from wrapper; place in large
bowl. Let dough stand at room temperature
about 15 minutes.

3. Add cocoa to dough; beat at medium speed
of electric mixer until well blended. Shape
dough into 18 balls; press onto bottoms and
up sides of prepared muffin cups.

4. Bake 12 to 14 minutes or until set. Remove
from oven; gently press down center of each
cookie with back of teaspoon. Cool in pan
10 minutes. Remove cups from pan; cool
completely on wire rack.

5. Fill each cup with 1 to 2 tablespoons
pudding; sprinkle with cookie crumbs.
Garnish with gummy worms.

Makes 1½ dozen cookie cups

Tip: Chocolate cookie crumbs can be
purchased in the baking section of the
supermarket.

Peanut Butter Cup Bars

1½ cups all-purpose flour
1 teaspoon baking powder
1 teaspoon salt
⅔ cup IMPERIAL® Spread, softened
2 cups sugar
4 eggs
1 cup semi-sweet chocolate chips, melted
½ cup Skippy® Creamy Peanut Butter

Preheat oven to 350°F. Grease 13×9-inch
baking pan; set aside.

In medium bowl, combine flour, baking
powder and salt; set aside.

In large bowl, with electric mixer, beat
Imperial Spread and sugar on medium-high
speed until light and fluffy, about 5 minutes.
Beat in eggs, scraping sides occasionally.
Gradually beat in flour mixture until blended.
Remove 2 cups batter to medium bowl and stir
in melted chocolate. Evenly spread batter into
prepared pan. Add Peanut Butter to remaining
batter in large bowl; beat until blended. Spoon
over chocolate batter and spread into even
layer.

Bake uncovered 35 minutes or until center is
set. On wire rack, cool completely. To serve,
cut into bars. *Makes 2 dozen bars*

Prep Time: 15 minutes
Cook Time: 35 minutes

Mice Creams

1 pint vanilla ice cream

1 (4-ounce) package READY CRUST® Mini-Graham Cracker Pie Crusts

Ears—12 KEEBLER® Grasshopper® cookies

Tails—3 chocolate twigs, broken in half *or* 6 (3-inch) pieces black shoestring licorice

Eyes and noses—18 brown candy-coated chocolate candies

Whiskers—2 teaspoons chocolate sprinkles

Place 1 scoop vanilla ice cream into each crust. Press cookie ears and tails into ice cream. Press eyes, noses and whiskers in place. Serve immediately. Do not refreeze.

Makes 6 servings

Prep Time: 15 minutes

Frozen Fudge Pops

½ cup nonfat sweetened condensed milk

¼ cup unsweetened cocoa powder

1¼ cups nonfat evaporated milk

1 teaspoon vanilla

1. Beat together sweetened condensed milk and cocoa in medium bowl. Add evaporated milk and vanilla; beat until smooth.

2. Pour mixture into 8 small paper cups or popsicle molds. Freeze about 2 hours or until almost firm. Insert wooden popsicle sticks into center of each cup; freeze until solid.

Makes 8 pops

Shamrock Parfaits

1 envelope unflavored gelatin

½ cup cold water

¾ cup sugar

½ cup HERSHEY'S Cocoa

1¼ cups evaporated nonfat milk

1 teaspoon vanilla extract

2 cups frozen light non-dairy whipped topping, thawed, divided

⅛ teaspoon mint extract

6 to 7 drops green food color

1. Sprinkle gelatin over water in medium bowl; let stand 2 minutes to soften. Cook over low heat, stirring constantly, until gelatin is completely dissolved, about 3 minutes. Stir together sugar and cocoa in small bowl; add gradually to gelatin mixture, stirring with whisk until well blended. Continue to cook over low heat, stirring constantly, until sugar is dissolved, about 3 minutes. Remove from heat. Stir in evaporated milk and vanilla. Pour mixture into large bowl. Refrigerate, stirring occasionally, until mixture mounds slightly when dropped from spoon, about 20 minutes.

2. Fold ½ cup whipped topping into chocolate mixture. Divide about half of mixture evenly among 8 parfait or wine glasses. Stir extract and food color into remaining 1½ cups topping; divide evenly among glasses. Spoon remaining chocolate mixture over topping in each glass. Garnish as desired. Serve immediately or cover and refrigerate until serving time.

Makes 8 servings

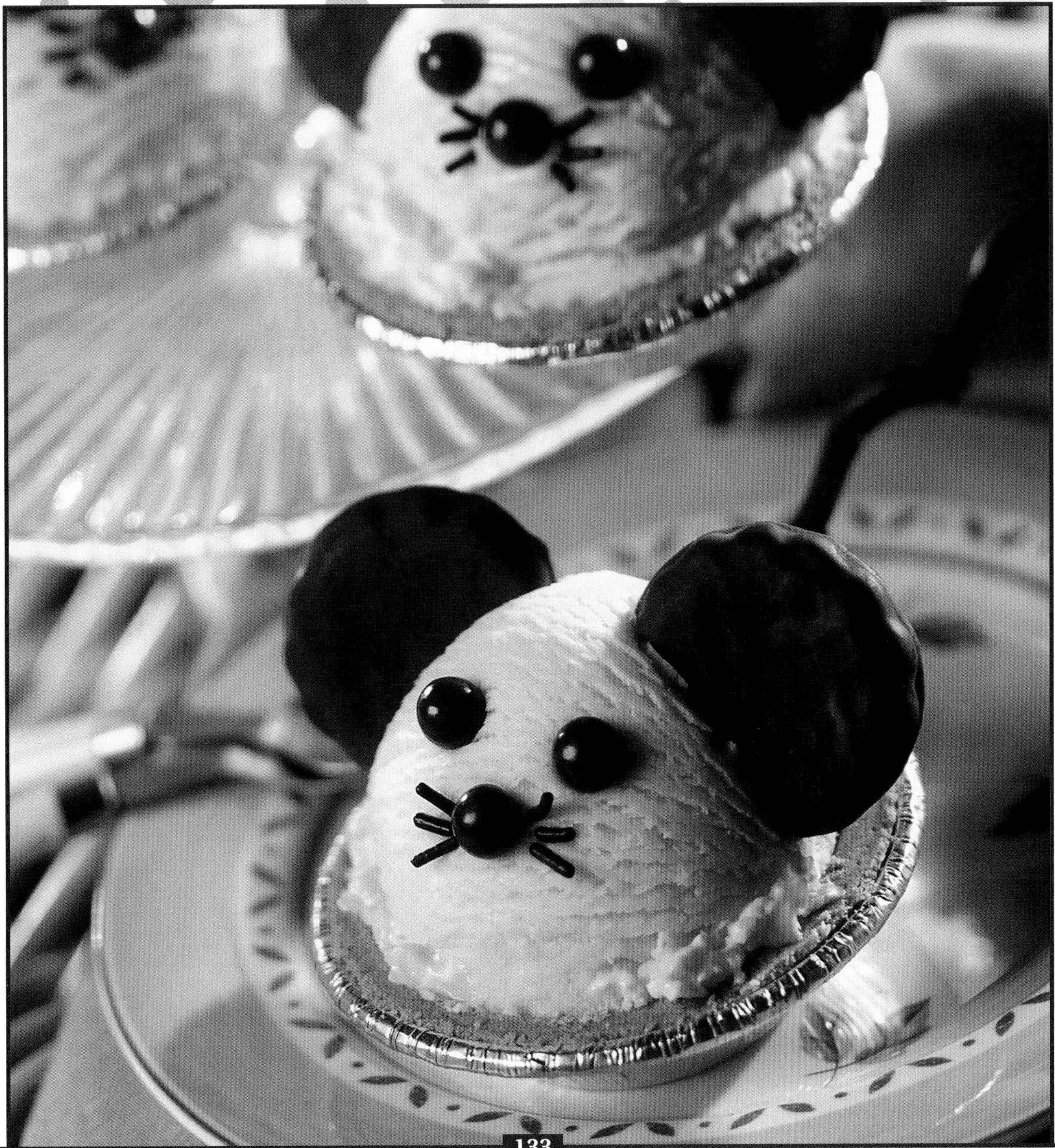

Cookie Pizza Cake

1 package (18 ounces) refrigerated
   chocolate chip cookie dough
1 package (18¼ ounces) chocolate cake
   mix, plus ingredients to prepare mix
1 cup prepared vanilla frosting
½ cup peanut butter
1 to 2 tablespoons milk
1 container (16 ounces) chocolate frosting
   Chocolate peanut butter cups, chopped

1. Preheat oven to 350°F. Coat two 12×1-inch round pizza pans with nonstick cooking spray. Press cookie dough evenly into one pan. Bake 15 to 20 minutes or until edges are golden brown. Cool 20 minutes in pan on wire rack. Remove from pan; cool completely.

2. Prepare cake mix according to package directions. Fill second pan ¼ to ½ full with batter.* Bake 10 to 15 minutes or until toothpick inserted into center comes out clean. Cool 15 minutes on wire rack. Gently remove cake from pan; cool completely.

3. Combine vanilla frosting and peanut butter in small bowl. Gradually stir in milk, 1 tablespoon at a time, until mixture is spreadable.

4. Place cookie on serving plate. Spread peanut butter frosting over cookie. Place cake on top of cookie, trimming cookie to match the size of cake, if necessary. Frost top and side of cake with chocolate frosting. Garnish with peanut butter cups.   *Makes 12 to 14 servings*

Discard remaining batter or use it to make cupcakes or another shaped cake. Do not let batter sit too long or it will not rise properly.

Stuffed Banana Smiles

1 medium size banana, with peel on
1 tablespoon SUN-MAID® Raisins or
   Golden Raisins
1 tablespoon semi-sweet, milk or white
   chocolate baking chips

1. **PLACE** banana, with peel on, flat on its side on a microwave-safe plate.

2. **STARTING*** and ending ¼ inch from the ends of banana, cut a slit lengthwise through the banana up to the skin on the other side.

3. **GENTLY** open the banana. Use your fingers to stuff the banana with raisins, then add chocolate chips.

4. **MICROWAVE*** banana uncovered on HIGH for 40 to 60 seconds or until chocolate begins to melt and banana is still firm. Banana skin may darken slightly. Eat immediately, scooping with a spoon right out of the banana peel.
          Makes 1 serving

Adult Supervision Suggested

Tip: At a party, invite guests to prepare their own banana smile!

Tip: Place wrapped bananas on a baking sheet and bake in the oven* at 350°F for 5 minutes.

Prep Time: 2 minutes
Bake Time: 1 minute

Cookie Pizza Cake

Frozen Berry Ice Cream

8 ounces frozen unsweetened
strawberries, partially thawed

8 ounces frozen unsweetened peaches,
partially thawed

4 ounces frozen unsweetened blueberries,
partially thawed

6 packets sugar substitute

2 teaspoons vanilla

2 cups vanilla ice cream

16 blueberries

4 small strawberries, halved

8 peach slices

1. Combine partially thawed strawberries,
peaches, blueberries, sugar substitute and
vanilla in food processor. Process until
coarsely chopped.

2. Add ice cream; process until well blended.

3. Serve immediately for semi-soft texture
or freeze until ready to serve. (If frozen, let
stand 10 minutes to soften slightly.) Garnish
each serving with 2 blueberries for "eyes,"
1 strawberry half for "nose" and 1 peach slice
for "smile."   *Makes 8 (½-cup) servings*

Trick-or-Treat Caramel Apples

1 package (14 ounces) chocolate
caramels*

1 cup miniature marshmallows

1 tablespoon water

5 or 6 medium apples

5 or 6 wooden craft sticks

Candy corn, red cinnamon candies,
jelly beans, licorice whips, colored
sprinkles and other assorted candies
for decoration

Can be made with any flavor caramels.

1. Place baking cups on baking sheet. Flatten
cups.

2. Combine caramels, marshmallows and
water in medium saucepan. Cook over
medium heat, stirring constantly, until
caramels melt.

3. Rinse and thoroughly dry apples. Insert
wooden sticks into stem ends.

4. Dip apple into caramel mixture, coating
thoroughly. Remove excess caramel mixture by
scraping apple bottom across rim of saucepan.
Place on baking cup.

5. Immediately decorate with candies to create
face or other design. (Work quickly or caramel
may harden and decorations will not adhere.)
Repeat with remaining apples. Refrigerate
until firm.   *Makes 5 or 6 servings*

Valentine Surprise

Pink and white decorating icings

18 whole plain graham crackers or chocolate-flavored graham crackers

6 scoops (about ½ cup each) strawberry ice cream or frozen yogurt

Assorted valentine candies, jelly beans or small fresh flowers

1. Spoon icings into pastry bags fitted with decorating tips; set aside.

2. Break graham crackers crosswise in half. Place 1 (½-cup) scoop ice cream in center of each of 6 graham cracker halves.

3. To form sides of each box, stand up one graham cracker half along each of the 4 sides of each graham cracker half topped with ice cream; pipe icing along seams to secure crackers in place. Make tops of boxes with remaining 6 graham cracker halves; pipe icing along remaining seams to secure in place.

4. Decorate boxes as desired with icing and candies, using icing to secure candies to crackers. Freeze until ready to serve. Freeze any leftovers. *Makes 6 servings*

Caramel Apples

2 cups heavy cream

2 cups sugar

¼ Butter Flavor CRISCO® Stick or ¼ cup Butter Flavor CRISCO® Shortening

½ cup dark corn syrup

12 medium McIntosh apples, washed and stemmed

12 wooden craft sticks

Line baking sheet with parchment paper; set aside. Fill about half of a large bowl with ice water.

Place cream, sugar, CRISCO® Shortening and corn syrup in a heavy-bottomed saucepan; bring to a boil over medium heat. Continue cooking until the temperature registers 245°F on a candy thermometer, 10 to 12 minutes. Remove from heat and briefly plunge the saucepan into ice water to stop the caramel from cooking. Remove from ice water and let mixture cool for a few minutes.

Insert a craft stick into the stem end of each apple. Dip 1 apple into the caramel; coat the top and sides with caramel using a spoon. Transfer to prepared baking sheet to cool. Repeat with remaining apples.

Makes 12 apples

Optional Toppings: Chocolate covered toffee bits, crushed Macadamia nuts, crushed peanuts, seasonal sprinkles, tinted coconut or chopped candy corn.

Note: Use 5-inch craft sticks, ¼-inch in diameter. Garnish as desired, or serve in seasonal cupcake liners.

The Finish Line

Cookie Fondue

Cookie Dippers

> 1 package (18 ounces) refrigerated oatmeal raisin cookie dough
>
> 1 cup powdered sugar
>
> 1 egg

Chocolate Sauce

> ½ cup semisweet chocolate chips
>
> ¼ cup heavy cream

White Chocolate Sauce

> ½ cup white chocolate chips
>
> ¼ cup heavy cream

Strawberry-Marshmallow Sauce

> ¼ cup strawberry syrup
>
> ¼ cup marshmallow creme

1. For cookie dippers, preheat oven to 350°F. Grease cookie sheets.

2. Remove dough from wrapper; place in large bowl. Let dough stand at room temperature about 15 minutes.

3. Add powdered sugar and egg to dough; beat at medium speed of electric mixer until well blended. Drop dough by teaspoonfuls onto prepared cookie sheets.

4. Bake 8 minutes or until edges are lightly browned. Cool on cookie sheets 5 minutes. Remove to wire rack; cool completely.

5. For chocolate sauce, combine semisweet chocolate chips and cream in microwavable bowl. Heat at HIGH (100% power) 20 seconds; stir. Heat at HIGH at additional 20-second intervals until chips are melted and mixture is smooth; stir well after each interval.

6. For white chocolate sauce, combine white chocolate chips and cream in microwavable bowl. Heat at HIGH (100% power) 20 seconds; stir. Heat at HIGH at additional 20-second intervals until chips are melted and mixture is smooth; stir well after each interval.

7. For strawberry-marshmallow sauce, mix strawberry syrup and marshmallow creme in small bowl; stir until smooth.

8. Serve cookie dippers with sauces.

Makes 2½ dozen cookies

Tip: Serve sauces in small bowls along with small bowls of chopped nuts, coconut and dried cranberries for "double" dipping.

Snackin' Banana Split

1 small ripe banana, peeled

1 small scoop vanilla frozen yogurt (about 3 tablespoons)

1 small scoop strawberry frozen yogurt (about 3 tablespoons)

⅓ cup sliced fresh strawberries or blueberries

2 tablespoons all-fruit strawberry fruit spread

1 teaspoon hot water

2 tablespoons low-fat granola cereal

1 maraschino cherry (optional)

1. Split banana in half lengthwise. Place in shallow bowl; top with frozen yogurt and strawberries.

2. Combine fruit spread and water in small bowl; mix well. Spoon over yogurt; sprinkle with granola. Top with cherry, if desired.

Makes 1 serving

Howlin' Good Party Treats

1 (4-pack) individual serving vanilla pudding

Food coloring (orange=4 drops red plus 8 drops yellow; green=12 drops green)

1 (4-ounce) package READY CRUST® Mini-Graham Cracker Pie Crusts

Famous Amos® cookies, broken into pieces

Mini marshmallows

Toasted coconut

Candy corn

Colored sprinkles

Cinnamon candies

Black licorice

Mini semi-sweet chocolate chips

Mini baking bits

1. Mix pudding with food coloring. Divide pudding between crusts.

2. Decorate with pieces of Famous Amos® cookies and other toppings as desired. Refrigerate leftovers. *Makes 6 servings*

Prep Time: 5 minutes

Snackin' Banana Split

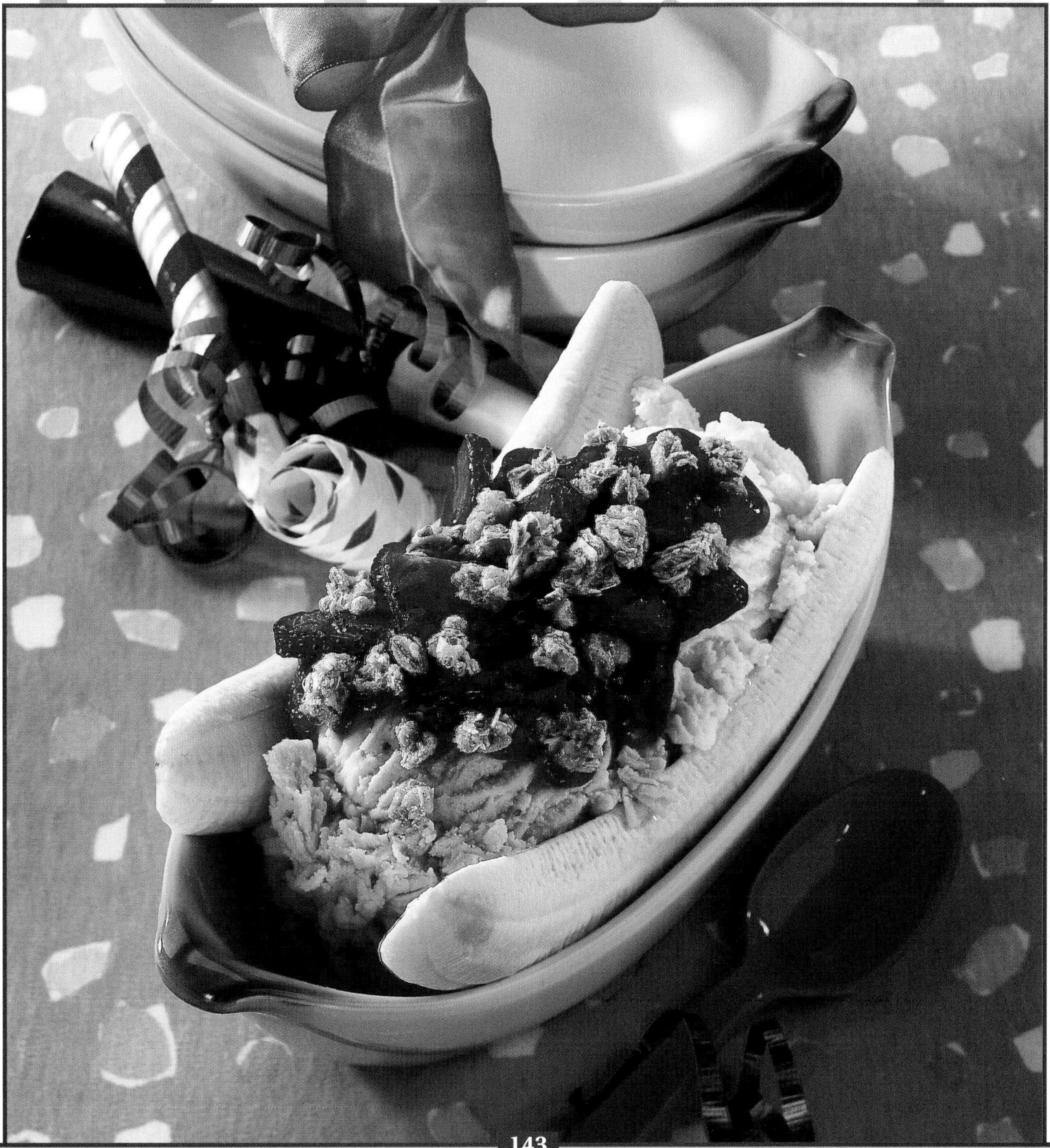

Slitherin' Centipede

1 package (20 ounces) refrigerated peanut butter cookie dough

1 container (16 ounces) chocolate frosting

  Black licorice whips, cut into 3-inch pieces

1 pink marshmallow and coconut covered chocolate snack cake

2 black jelly beans

  Red pull-apart licorice strings

1. Preheat oven to 350°F. Remove dough from wrapper and cut into 18 to 20 slices. Place slices 2 inches apart on greased cookies sheets.

2. Bake 8 to 10 minutes or until edges are lightly browned. Cool completely on wire racks.

3. In sections of 6 cookies at a time, sandwich cookies together with frosting. Insert licorice "legs" in frosting until all cookies are sandwiched together with frosting and licorice.

4. Attach cookie sections end-to-end on their sides on serving platter in a wavy pattern. Use frosting to attach sections together and add legs between all segments.

5. Attach snack cake to one end of centipede using frosting. Decorate snack cake with jelly bean eyes and red licorice antennae.

Makes 1 worm (18 to 20 cookies)

Tip: To make this scary creature into a cute birthday treat, use green jelly beans for eyes, brightly colored licorice for legs, and vanilla frosting between cookies. Insert birthday candles into the frosting..

Old-Fashioned Caramel Apples

1 package (14 ounces) caramels

2 tablespoons water

6 wooden craft sticks

6 medium Granny Smith apples

  Chopped toasted pecans, walnuts or roasted peanuts

  Orange and black jimmies or sprinkles

1. Place caramels and water in a medium heavy saucepan. Cook over medium-low heat until melted and very hot, stirring frequently.

2. Insert stick into stem end of each apple. Place pecans in shallow bowl and jimmies in another shallow bowl. Dip apple into caramel, tilting saucepan until apple is coated; let excess caramel drip back in saucepan. Remove excess caramel by scraping bottom of apple across rim of saucepan. Immediately roll apple in pecans and/or jimmies. Place, stick side up, on baking sheet lined with waxed paper. Repeat with remaining apples. Rewarm caramel, if needed. Chill at least 10 minutes or until caramel is firm before serving.

Makes 6 servings

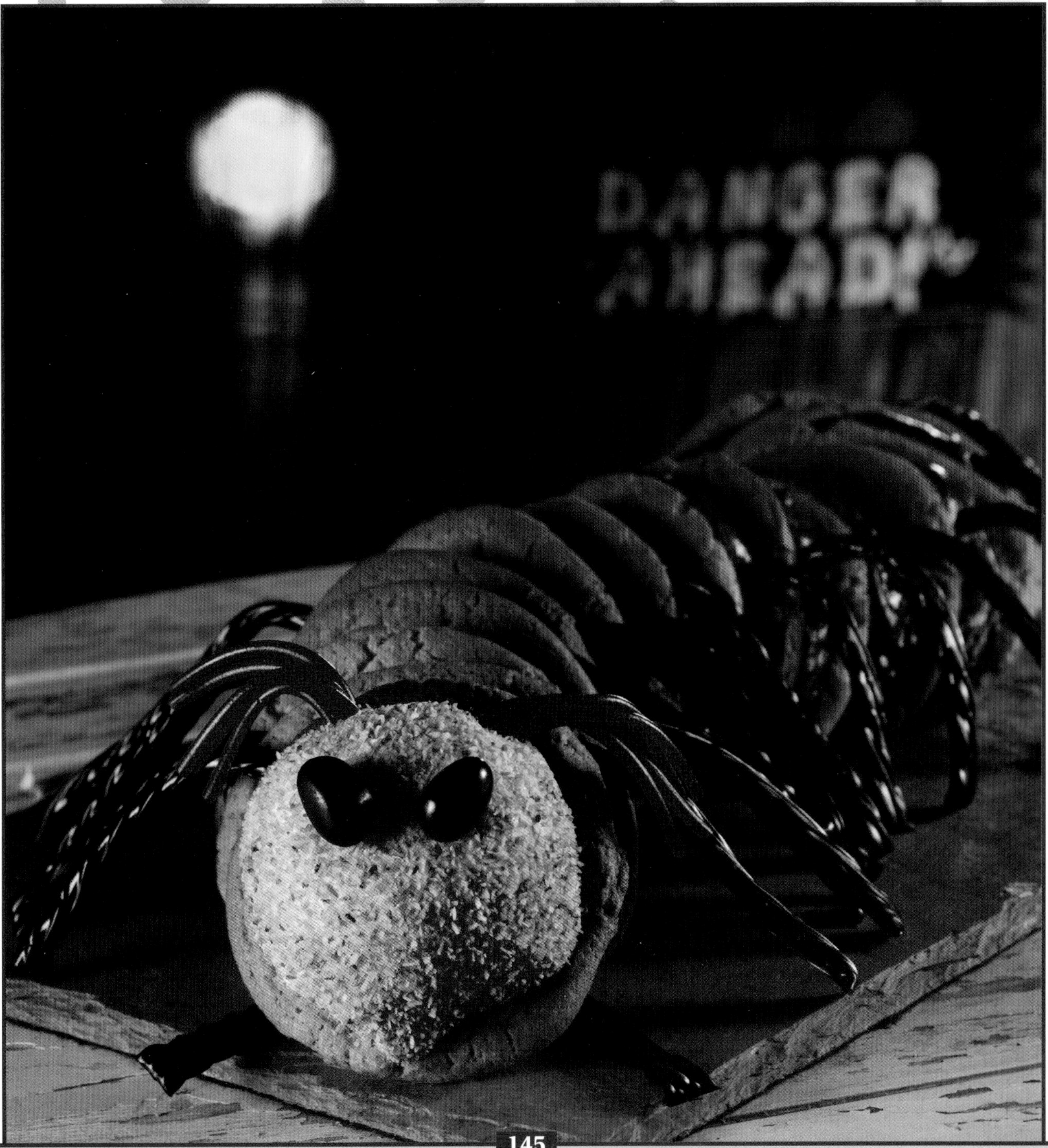
DANGER
AHEAD!

Creamy Strawberry-Orange Pops

1 container (8 ounces) strawberry yogurt

¾ cup orange juice

2 teaspoons vanilla

2 cups frozen whole strawberries

2 teaspoons sugar

6 (7-ounce) paper cups

6 wooden sticks

1. Combine yogurt, orange juice and vanilla in food processor or blender. Cover and blend until smooth.

2. Add frozen strawberries and sugar. Blend until smooth. Pour into 6 paper cups, filling each about ¾ full. Freeze 1 hour. Insert wooden stick into center of each. Freeze completely. Peel cup off each to serve.

Makes 6 servings

Crispy Chocolate Footballs

2 cups semisweet chocolate chips

½ cup light corn syrup

¼ cup (½ stick) butter

7 cups crisp rice cereal

Cookie Glaze (recipe follows)

1. Line baking sheets with waxed paper; set aside.

2. Combine chocolate chips, corn syrup and butter in medium saucepan. Cook and stir over low heat until chips are melted and mixture is smooth.

3. Place cereal in large bowl. Pour chocolate mixture over cereal; stir to coat evenly.

4. Lightly butter hands. Shape about ⅓ cup cereal mixture into football shapes, each about 2×1¼ inches. Place on prepared baking sheets.

5. Prepare Cookie Glaze. Using pastry bag fitted with writing tip, pipe lines and laces onto footballs.   *Makes about 20 footballs*

Cookie Glaze: Combine 1 cup powdered sugar and 1 tablespoon milk in small bowl. Stir in enough additional powdered sugar to glaze to make consistency suitable for piping.

Variation: Shape cereal mixture into one large football or press mixture into greased 13×9-inch baking pan and cut into squares.

Peanut Butter Ice Cream Triangles

1½ cups all-purpose flour

½ teaspoon baking powder

½ teaspoon baking soda

¼ teaspoon salt

½ cup (1 stick) butter, softened

½ cup granulated sugar

½ cup packed brown sugar

½ cup creamy peanut butter

1 egg

1 teaspoon vanilla

2½ to 3 cups vanilla, cinnamon or chocolate ice cream, softened

1. Preheat oven to 350°F. Grease cookie sheets.

2. Combine flour, baking powder, baking soda and salt in small bowl; set aside. Beat butter, granulated sugar and brown sugar in large bowl of electric mixer at medium speed until light and fluffy. Beat in peanut butter, egg and vanilla until well blended. Gradually beat in flour mixture on low speed until blended.

3. Divide dough in half. Roll each piece of dough between 2 sheets of waxed paper or plastic wrap into 10×10-inch square, about ⅛ inch thick. Remove top sheet of waxed paper; invert dough onto prepared cookie sheet. Remove second sheet of waxed paper.

4. Score dough into four 4-inch squares. Score each square diagonally into two triangles. *Do not cut completely through dough.* Repeat with remaining dough. Combine excess scraps of dough; roll out and score into additional triangles.

5. Bake 12 to 13 minutes or until set and edges are golden brown. Cool cookies 2 minutes on cookie sheets. Cut through score marks with knife; cool completely on cookie sheets.

6. Place half the cookies on flat surface. Spread ¼ to ⅓ cup softened ice cream on flat side of each cookie; top with remaining cookies. Wrap in plastic wrap and freeze 1 hour or up to 2 days.

Makes about 10 ice cream sandwiches

Backyard S'Mores

2 milk chocolate bars (1.55 ounces each), cut in half

8 large marshmallows

4 whole graham crackers (8 squares)

Place each chocolate bar half and 2 marshmallows between 2 graham cracker squares. Wrap in lightly greased foil. Place on grill over medium-low KINGSFORD® Briquets about 3 to 5 minutes or until chocolate and marshmallows are melted. (Time will vary depending upon how hot coals are and whether grill is open or covered.)

Makes 4 servings

Peanut Butter Ice Cream Triangles

Caramel Apple Wedges

⅔ cup sugar

¼ cup (½ stick) butter, cut into small pieces

½ cup whipping cream

¼ teaspoon salt

3 apples, cored, cut into 6 wedges each

½ cup shredded coconut

¼ cup mini chocolate chips

1. Place sugar in medium, heavy saucepan. Cook over low heat until sugar melts, about 20 minutes. Carefully stir in butter; stir in cream. (Mixture will spatter.) Cook over low heat until any lumps disappear, about 15 minutes, stirring occasionally. Stir in salt.

2. To serve, pour caramel sauce into serving bowl or fondue pot over heat source. Arrange apple wedges on a plate. Combine coconut and chocolate chips in serving bowl.

3. Using fondue forks, dip apple wedges into caramel sauce, then into coconut mixture.

Makes 6 servings

Chocolate Peanut Butter Fondue

⅓ cup unsweetened cocoa powder

⅓ cup sugar

⅓ cup low-fat (1%) milk

3 tablespoons light corn syrup

2 tablespoons reduced-fat peanut butter

½ teaspoon vanilla

2 medium bananas, cut into 1-inch pieces

16 large strawberries

2 medium apples, cored, sliced

1. Mix cocoa, sugar, milk, corn syrup and peanut butter in medium saucepan. Cook over medium heat, stirring constantly, until hot. Remove from heat; stir in vanilla.

2. Pour fondue into medium serving bowl; serve warm or at room temperature with fruit for dipping.

Makes 8 servings

Chocolate-Caramel S'Mores

12 chocolate wafer cookies or chocolate graham cracker squares

2 tablespoons caramel ice cream topping

6 large marshmallows

1. Prepare coals for grilling. Place 6 wafer cookies top down on plate. Spread 1 teaspoon caramel topping in center of each wafer to within about ¼ inch of edge.

2. Spear 1 to 2 marshmallows onto long wood-handled skewer.* Hold several inches above coals 3 to 5 minutes or until marshmallows are golden and very soft, turning slowly. Push 1 marshmallow off into center of caramel. Top with plain wafer. Repeat with remaining marshmallows and wafers.

Makes 6 servings

If wood-handled skewers are unavailable, use oven mitt to protect hand from heat.

Tip: S'Mores, a favorite campfire treat, got their name because everyone who tasted them wanted "some more." In the unlikely event of leftover S'Mores, they can be reheated in the microwave at HIGH 5 to 10 seconds.

Friendly Ghost Puffs

1 cup water

½ cup (1 stick) butter, cut into pieces

1 cup all-purpose flour

¼ teaspoon salt

4 eggs

1 quart orange sherbet

Powdered sugar

16 chocolate chips

1. Bring water and butter to a boil in medium saucepan over high heat, stirring until butter is melted. Reduce heat to low; stir in flour and salt until mixture forms a ball. Remove from heat. Add eggs, one at a time, beating after each addition until mixture is smooth.

2. Preheat oven to 400°F. Spoon about ⅓ cup dough onto ungreased baking sheet. With wet knife, form into ghost shape 3 inches wide and 4 inches long. Repeat with remaining dough to form ghosts, spacing them about 2 inches apart.

3. Bake 40 to 45 minutes or until puffed and golden. Remove to wire racks; cool completely.

4. Carefully cut each ghost in half horizontally; remove soft interior leaving hollow shell.

5. Just before serving, fill each shell bottom with about ½ cup orange sherbet. Cover with top of shell; sprinkle with powdered sugar. Position 2 chocolate chips on each ghost for eyes.

Makes 8 servings

Charmed Circles

1 Granny Smith or Jonathan apple, peeled

¼ teaspoon cherry-flavored gelatin

2 tablespoons cherry cola

2 tablespoons thawed frozen nondairy whipped topping

2 mini chocolate chips

1. Slice apple crosswise into ¼-inch-thick rings. Sprinkle gelatin in microwavable pie plate. Dip apple rings in gelatin to coat and place in single layer in pie plate. Pour cola around rings.

2. Cover loosely with waxed paper. Microwave at HIGH 1 minute or until liquid is boiling. Allow to stand, covered, 5 minutes. Arrange rings on dessert plate. Pipe on whipped topping ghost and add chocolate chip eyes. Serve warm or at room temperature.

Makes 1 serving

Note: To cook 2 apples at a time, increase cooking time to 2½ minutes. For 3 apples at a time, cook 4 minutes.

Fruity S'mores

1½ packages (16 ounces each) refrigerated sugar or chocolate chip cookie dough or 40 bakery cookies

Colored sugar (optional)

1 cup marshmallow creme

4 ounces whipped cream cheese

1 can (15 ounces) DOLE® Mandarin Oranges, drained

• Slice and bake cookies (if using) as directed on package; cool. If desired, before baking cookies sprinkle with colored sugar.

• Stir together marshmallow creme and cream cheese until well blended.

• Assemble each s'more by spreading 1 tablespoon marshmallow creme mixture over bottom of one cookie. Sprinkle a few mandarin oranges over creme; top with second cookie. Repeat with remaining cookies. Serve immediately. *Makes 20 servings*

Prep Time: 15 minutes
Bake Time: 11 minutes

Chocolate Halloween Ice Cream Sandwiches

2 cups all-purpose flour

½ cup unsweetened cocoa powder

2 teaspoons baking soda

½ teaspoon salt

1¼ cups sugar

⅔ cup butter, softened

¼ cup light corn syrup

1 egg

1 teaspoon vanilla

3 pints mint chocolate chip and/or vanilla ice cream

Black and orange sprinkles, sugar or other Halloween cookie decorations (optional)

1. Preheat oven to 350°F. Combine flour, cocoa, baking soda and salt in medium bowl. Beat sugar and butter in large bowl of electric mixer on medium speed until light and fluffy. Beat in corn syrup, egg and vanilla until well blended. Gradually beat in flour mixture at low speed until blended. Cover and refrigerate dough about 15 minutes or until firm.

2. Roll dough into 1-inch balls, using about 1 tablespoon dough per ball. Place balls 2 inches apart on *ungreased* cookie sheets. Press lightly with fingers to flatten slightly. Bake 10 to 12 minutes or until cookies are set. Immediately transfer to wire racks; cool completely.

3. Soften ice cream at room temperature about 10 minutes or in microwave at MEDIUM (50% power) 10 to 20 seconds. For each ice cream sandwich, place about ¼ cup (1 small scoop) ice cream on flat side of a cookie; top with another cookie, flat side down. Press gently so that ice cream meets edges of cookies. Immediately roll edges of ice cream in decorations, if desired. Wrap in plastic wrap; freeze until ready to serve.

Makes about 2 dozen sandwiches

Orange Pudding Cones

1 package (4-serving size) chocolate or vanilla instant pudding

1¾ cups cold milk

8 ice cream cones (with flat bottoms)

1 can (11 ounces) DOLE® Mandarin Oranges, drained

Candy or chocolate sprinkles (optional)

• Stir together pudding and milk for 2 minutes until smooth and blended.

• Fill cones halfway with pudding; sprinkle two mandarin oranges over pudding in each cup. Add a few more spoonfuls of pudding. Garnish top of each cone with two or three mandarin oranges.

• Sprinkle with candy or chocolate sprinkles, if desired. Serve immediately.

Makes 8 servings

Prep Time: 5 minutes

Candy Corn Crispie Treats

½ cup (1 stick) butter

9 cups miniature marshmallows

10 cups chocolate crisp rice cereal

2 cups candy corn

¾ cup miniature chocolate chips

Assorted candy pumpkins

1. Melt butter in large saucepan over medium heat. Add marshmallows and stir until smooth.

2. Combine cereal, candy corn and chocolate chips in large bowl. Pour marshmallow mixture over cereal mixture, stirring quickly to coat. For best results, use a wooden spoon sprayed with nonstick cooking spray.

3. Spread mixture on large buttered jelly-roll pan, pressing out evenly with buttered hands. While still warm, press on candy pumpkins spaced about 1½ inches apart.

4. Cool completely; cut into squares.

Makes about 48 squares

Rocky Road Pudding

½ cup sugar

5 tablespoons unsweetened cocoa powder

3 tablespoons cornstarch

⅛ teaspoon salt

2½ cups low-fat (1%) milk

2 egg yolks, beaten

2 teaspoons vanilla

1 cup miniature marshmallows

¼ cup chopped walnuts, toasted

1. Combine sugar, cocoa, cornstarch and salt in small saucepan; mix well. Stir in milk; cook over medium-high heat, stirring constantly, about 10 minutes or until mixture thickens and begins to boil.

2. Pour about ½ cup pudding mixture over beaten egg yolks in small bowl; beat well. Pour mixture back into saucepan. Cook over medium heat an additional 10 minutes. Remove from heat; stir in vanilla.

3. Place plastic wrap on surface of pudding. Refrigerate about 20 minutes or until slightly cooled. Spoon pudding into 6 dessert dishes; top with marshmallows and nuts. Serve warm or cold.

Makes 6 servings

Candy Corn Crispie Treats

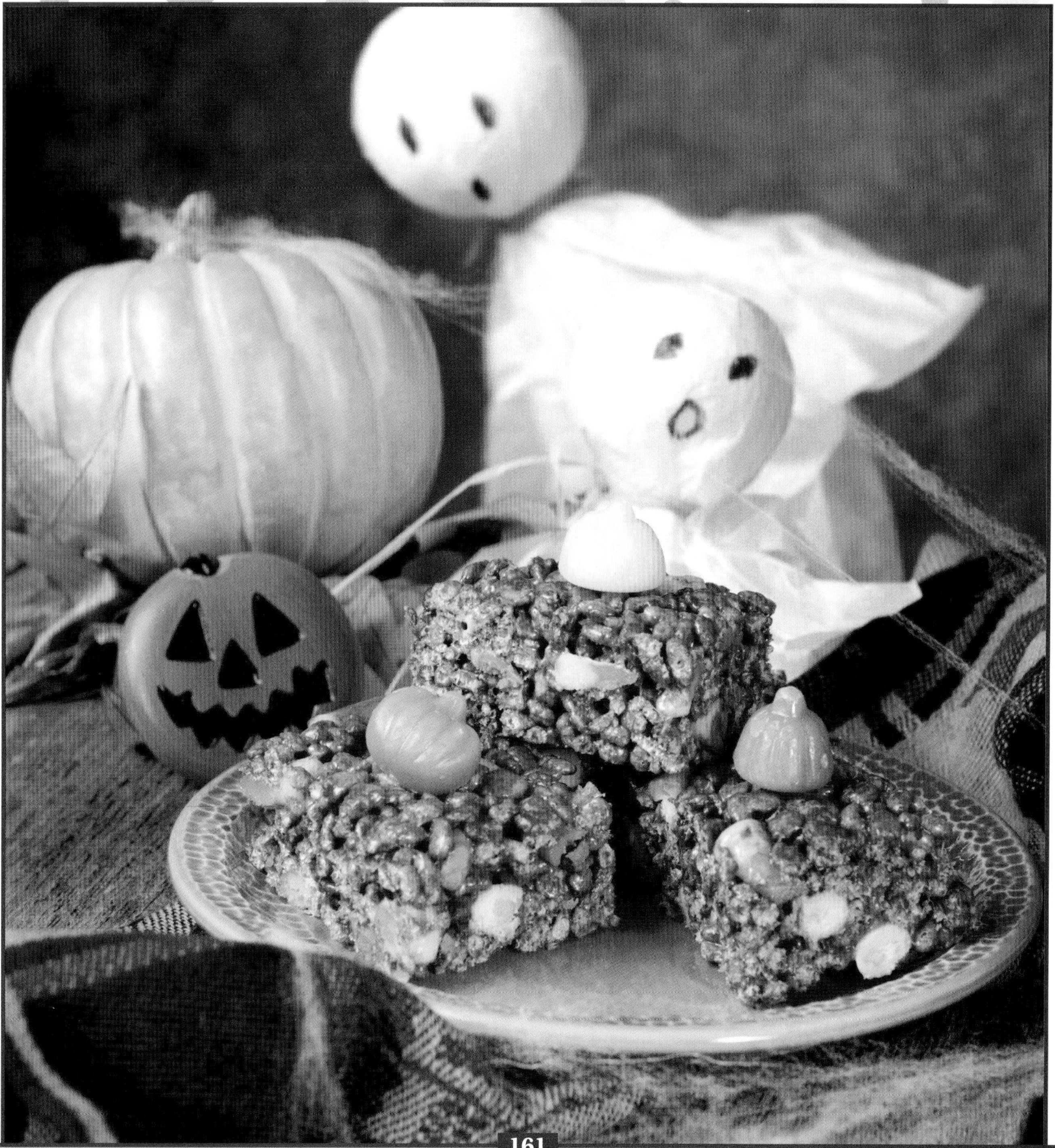

Football Bears

1¼ cups water

½ cup (1 stick) butter

1¼ cups all-purpose flour

⅛ teaspoon salt

5 eggs

1¼ cups prepared vanilla pudding

1 package (12 ounces) butterscotch chips

3 tablespoons shortening

Powdered sugar

Cookie Glaze (recipe follows)

Mini semisweet chocolate chips

Candy-coated chocolate pieces

Assorted food colorings

1. Bring water and butter to a boil in medium saucepan. Add flour and salt; stir until dough forms a ball. Remove from heat; beat in eggs, 1 at a time, with wooden spoon or wire whisk until dough is smooth and shiny.

2. Preheat oven to 400°F. Line baking sheet with parchment paper. Using pastry bag fitted with large writing tip, pipe dough into 3×1½-inch oval on prepared baking sheet for body. Repeat to make 11 additional ovals, spacing ovals about 2 inches apart.

3. Pipe ¾-inch rounds for heads and four ½-inch rounds for legs and arms for each bear. Pipe small round at base of each head for snout and 2 small dots at top of each head for ears.

4. Bake 10 minutes. Reduce heat to 350°F. Bake 25 to 30 minutes or until golden brown. Carefully remove bears to wire racks; cool completely.

5. Using serrated knife, slice off top of rounded stomach on each bear. Scoop out soft dough; discard. Spoon pudding evenly into stomach cavities; replace tops of stomachs. Place bears on wire rack over waxed paper.

6. Melt butterscotch chips with shortening in top of double boiler over hot water, stirring until smooth; spoon over bears, spreading to coat evenly. Refrigerate 10 minutes or until coating is firm.

7. Use small dabs of glaze to attach chocolate chips for eyes and candy pieces for noses. Remove about ¼ of Cookie Glaze for decorating shirts. Tint as desired and spoon into pastry bag fitted with small writing tip; set aside.

8. Color remaining glaze as desired; spread onto fronts of bears to resemble shirts. Using frosting in pastry bag, pipe stripes and numbers on shirts to resemble football jerseys. Refrigerate until ready to serve. Refrigerate any leftovers. *Makes 12 bears*

Cookie Glaze: Combine 4 cups powdered sugar and 4 tablespoons milk in small bowl. Add enough powdered sugar for proper piping consistency.

Football Bears and Crispy Chocolate Footballs (page 146)

Cookie Sundae Cups

1 package (18 ounces) refrigerated chocolate chip cookie dough

6 cups ice cream, any flavor

1¼ cups ice cream topping, any flavor

Whipped cream

Colored sprinkles

1. Preheat oven to 350°F. Lightly grease 18 standard (2½-inch) muffin pan cups.

2. Remove dough from wrapper. Shape dough into 18 balls; press onto bottoms and up sides of prepared muffin cups.

3. Bake 14 to 18 minutes or until golden brown. Cool in muffin cups 10 minutes. Remove to wire rack; cool completely.

4. Place ⅓ cup ice cream in each cookie cup. Drizzle with ice cream topping. Top with whipped cream and colored sprinkles.

Makes 1½ dozen desserts

Ice Cream Sandwiches

1 package (18¼ ounces) chocolate cake mix with pudding in the mix

2 eggs

¼ cup warm water

3 tablespoons butter, melted

1 pint vanilla ice cream, softened

Decorative sugar sprinkles or jimmies

1. Preheat oven to 350°F. Lightly spray 13×9-inch pan with nonstick cooking spray. Line pan with heavy-duty foil; spray foil.

2. Beat cake mix, eggs, water and melted butter in large bowl with electric mixer until well blended. (Dough will be thick and sticky.) Spoon dough into prepared pan. Cover with plastic wrap and press dough evenly into pan, using plastic wrap to keep hands from sticking to dough. Remove plastic wrap and prick surface all over with fork (about 40 times) to prevent dough from rising too much.

3. Bake 20 minutes or until toothpick inserted into center comes out clean. Cool in pan on wire rack.

4. Cut cookie in half crosswise; remove one half from pan. Spread ice cream evenly over cookie half remaining in pan. Top with second half; use foil in pan to wrap up sandwich.

5. Freeze at least 4 hours. Cut into 8 equal pieces; dip cut ends in sugar or sprinkles. Wrap sandwiches individually and freeze until ready to serve.

Makes 8 sandwiches

Peppermint Ice Cream Sandwiches: Stir ⅓ cup crushed peppermint candies into vanilla ice cream before assembling. Roll ends of sandwiches in additional crushed peppermint candies to coat.

Tip: If the ice cream is too hard to scoop easily, microwave at HIGH 10 seconds to soften.

Cookie Sundae Cup

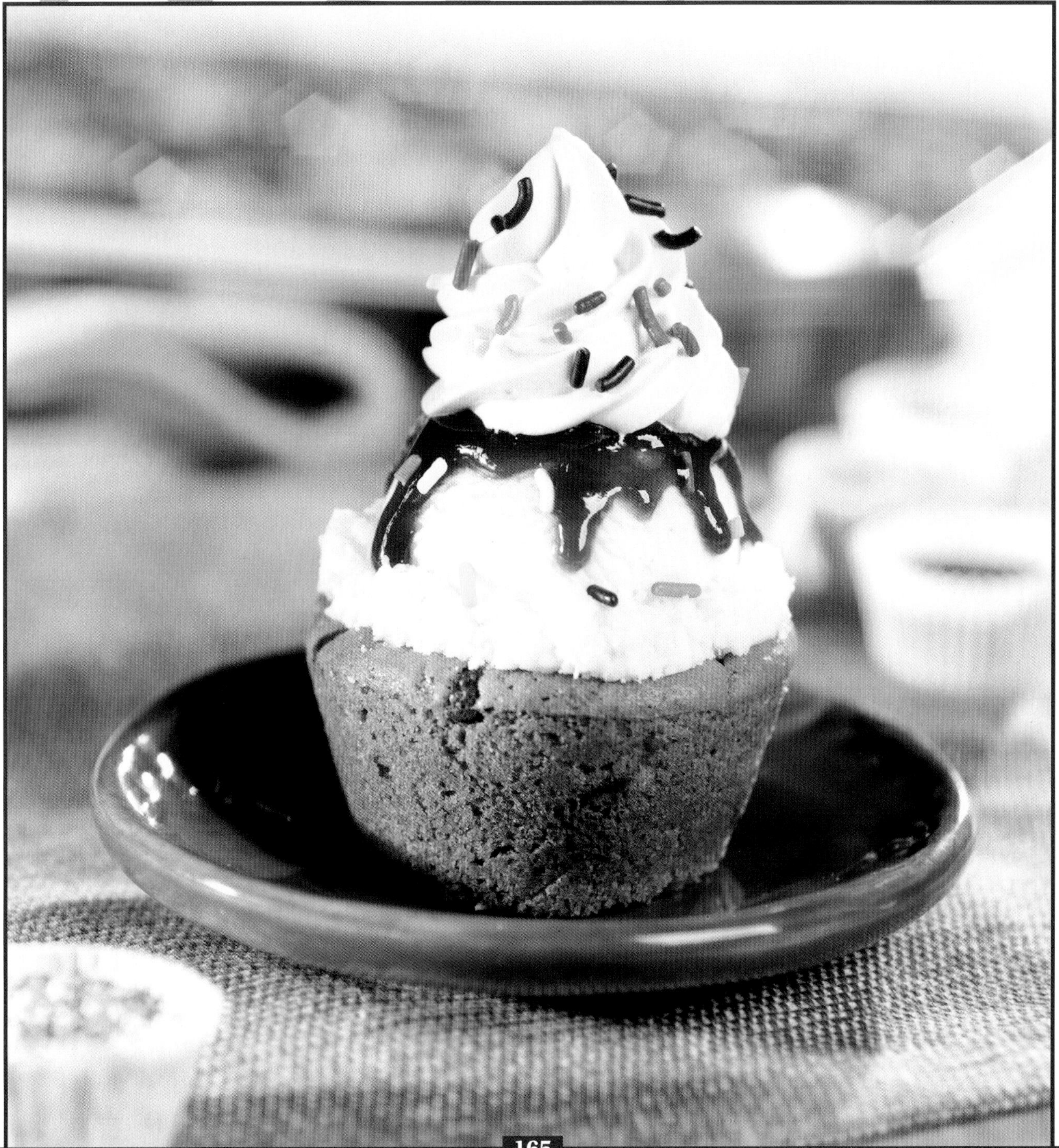

Microwave Chocolate Pudding

⅓ cup sugar

¼ cup unsweetened cocoa powder

2 tablespoons cornstarch

1½ cups reduced-fat (2%) milk

1 teaspoon vanilla

⅛ teaspoon ground cinnamon (optional)

Assorted small candies (optional)

1. Combine sugar, cocoa powder and cornstarch in medium microwavable bowl or 1-quart glass measure. Gradually add milk, stirring with wire whisk until well blended.

2. Microwave at HIGH (100% power) 2 minutes; stir. Microwave at MEDIUM-HIGH (70% power) 3½ to 4½ minutes or until thickened, stirring every 1½ minutes.

3. Stir in vanilla and cinnamon, if desired. Let stand at least 5 minutes before serving, stirring occasionally to prevent skin from forming. Serve warm or chilled. Garnish with candies just before serving, if desired.

Makes 4 (⅓-cup) servings

Black Lagoon

2 cups light or rock-colored jelly beans

1 package (6 ounces) blue gelatin

1 cup boiling water

1 cup cold concentrated grape juice

1 cup ice cubes

Gummy fish

Fresh parsley sprigs or celery leaves

Canned whipped cream (optional)

1. Place jelly beans in 9-inch glass pie plate; tilt until beans mound on one side to resemble a "shoreline."

2. Pour gelatin in medium bowl and add boiling water. Stir 2 minutes to dissolve completely. Add grape juice and ice cubes; stir until ice cubes have melted. Pour slowly into empty side of pie plate, holding back jelly beans with spoon.

3. Refrigerate until gelatin just begins to set. When gelatin has partially set, use a skewer to place gummy fish and parsley sprigs as seaweed. If desired, create a foamy shoreline with whipped cream along edge of jelly beans.

Makes 6 to 8 servings

Variation: For an extra-creepy lagoon, add green gelatin to blue gelatin for sickly color. Add circle candies for old tires, wilted frisée lettuce greens at bottom, and float fish on top of water.

Bar Cookies

Ooey-Gooey Caramel Peanut Butter Bars

1 package (18¼ ounces) yellow cake mix *without* pudding in the mix

1 cup uncooked quick-cooking oats

⅔ cup creamy peanut butter

1 egg, slightly beaten

2 tablespoons milk

1 package (8 ounces) cream cheese, softened

1 jar (12¼ ounces) caramel ice cream topping

1 cup semisweet chocolate chips

1. Preheat oven to 350°F. Lightly grease 13×9-inch baking pan.

2. Combine cake mix and oats in large bowl. Cut in peanut butter with pastry blender or 2 knives until mixture is crumbly.

3. Blend egg and milk in small bowl. Add to peanut butter mixture; stir just until combined. Reserve 1½ cups mixture. Press remaining peanut butter mixture into prepared pan.

4. Beat cream cheese in small bowl with electric mixer on medium speed until fluffy. Add caramel topping; beat just until combined. Carefully spread over peanut butter mixture in pan. Crumble reserved peanut butter mixture; sprinkle over cream cheese layer. Top with chocolate chips.

5. Bake about 30 minutes or until nearly set in center. Cool completely on wire rack.

Makes 24 bars

Ooey-Gooey Caramel Peanut Butter Bars

Peanut Butter Pizza Cookies

1¼ **cups firmly packed light brown sugar**

¾ **cup JIF® Creamy Peanut Butter**

½ **CRISCO® Stick or ½ cup CRISCO®**
   all-vegetable shortening

3 **tablespoons milk**

1 **tablespoon vanilla**

1 **egg**

1¾ **cups all-purpose flour**

¾ **teaspoon salt**

¾ **teaspoon baking soda**

8 **ounces white baking chocolate, chopped**
   Decorative candies

1. Heat oven to 375°F. Place sheets of foil on countertop for cooling cookies.

2. Combine brown sugar, peanut butter, ½ cup shortening, milk and vanilla in large bowl. Beat at medium speed of electric mixer until well blended. Add egg. Beat just until blended.

3. Combine flour, salt and baking soda. Add to creamed mixture at low speed. Mix just until blended.

4. Divide dough in half. Form each half into a ball. Place 1 ball of dough onto center of ungreased pizza pan or baking sheet. Spread dough with fingers to form 12-inch circle. Repeat with remaining ball of dough.

5. Bake one baking sheet at a time at 375°F for 10 to 12 minutes, or until lightly browned. *Do not overbake.* Cool 2 minutes on baking sheet. Remove with large spatula to foil to cool completely.

6. Place white chocolate in shallow microwave-safe bowl. Microwave on 100% (HIGH) for 30 seconds. Stir. Repeat at 30-second intervals until white chocolate is melted.

7. Spread melted white chocolate on center of cooled cookies to within ½ inch of edge. Decorate with candies. Let set completely. Cut into wedges.   *Makes 2 pizzas*

Chocolate Peanutty Crumble Bars

½ **cup butter or margarine**

1 **cup all-purpose flour**

¾ **cup instant oats, uncooked**

⅓ **cup firmly packed brown sugar**

½ **teaspoon baking soda**

½ **teaspoon vanilla extract**

4 **SNICKERS® Bars (2.07 ounces each), cut**
   into 8 slices each

Preheat oven to 350°F. Grease bottom of an 8-inch square pan. Melt butter in large saucepan. Remove from heat and stir in flour, oats, brown sugar, baking soda and vanilla. Blend until crumbly. Press ⅔ of the mixture into prepared pan. Arrange SNICKERS® Bar slices in pan, about ½ inch from the edge of pan. Finely crumble the remaining mixture over the sliced SNICKERS® Bars. Bake for 25 minutes or until edges are golden brown. Cool in pan on cooling rack. Cut into bars or squares to serve.   *Makes 24 bars*

S'More Bars

1 package (18 ounces) refrigerated
    chocolate chip cookie dough
¼ cup graham cracker crumbs
3 cups mini marshmallows
½ cup semisweet or milk chocolate chips
2 teaspoons shortening

1. Preheat oven to 350°F. Grease 13×9×2-inch baking pan.

2. Remove dough from wrapper. Press dough into prepared pan. Sprinkle evenly with graham cracker crumbs.

3. Bake 10 to 12 minutes or until edges are golden brown. Sprinkle with marshmallows. Bake 2 to 3 minutes or until marshmallows are puffed. Cool completely on wire rack.

4. Combine chocolate chips and shortening in small resealable plastic food storage bag; seal. Microwave at HIGH (100% power) 1 minute; knead bag lightly. Microwave at HIGH for additional 30-second intervals until chips and shortening are completely melted and smooth, kneading bag after each 30-second interval. Cut off small corner of bag. Drizzle chocolate over bars. Refrigerate 5 to 10 minutes or until chocolate is set.   *Makes 3 dozen bars*

Easy Layered Bars

½ cup (1 stick) butter, melted
1½ cups graham cracker crumbs
1 can (14 ounces) sweetened condensed
    milk
½ cup coconut
1 cup peanut butter chips
1¼ cups crisp rice cereal
1 cup semisweet chocolate chips
½ cup candy-coated chocolate pieces or
    baking bits

1. Preheat oven to 350°F. Lightly spray sides of 13×9-inch baking pan with nonstick cooking spray. Pour butter into pan.

2. Sprinkle graham cracker crumbs over butter. Pour condensed milk evenly over crumbs. Sprinkle coconut and peanut butter chips in even layers, then cereal, chocolate chips and candy-coated chocolate pieces; press gently.

3. Bake 25 to 27 minutes or until top just begins to brown. Cool completely in pan on wire rack. Cut into bars.

Makes about 36 bars

S'More Bars

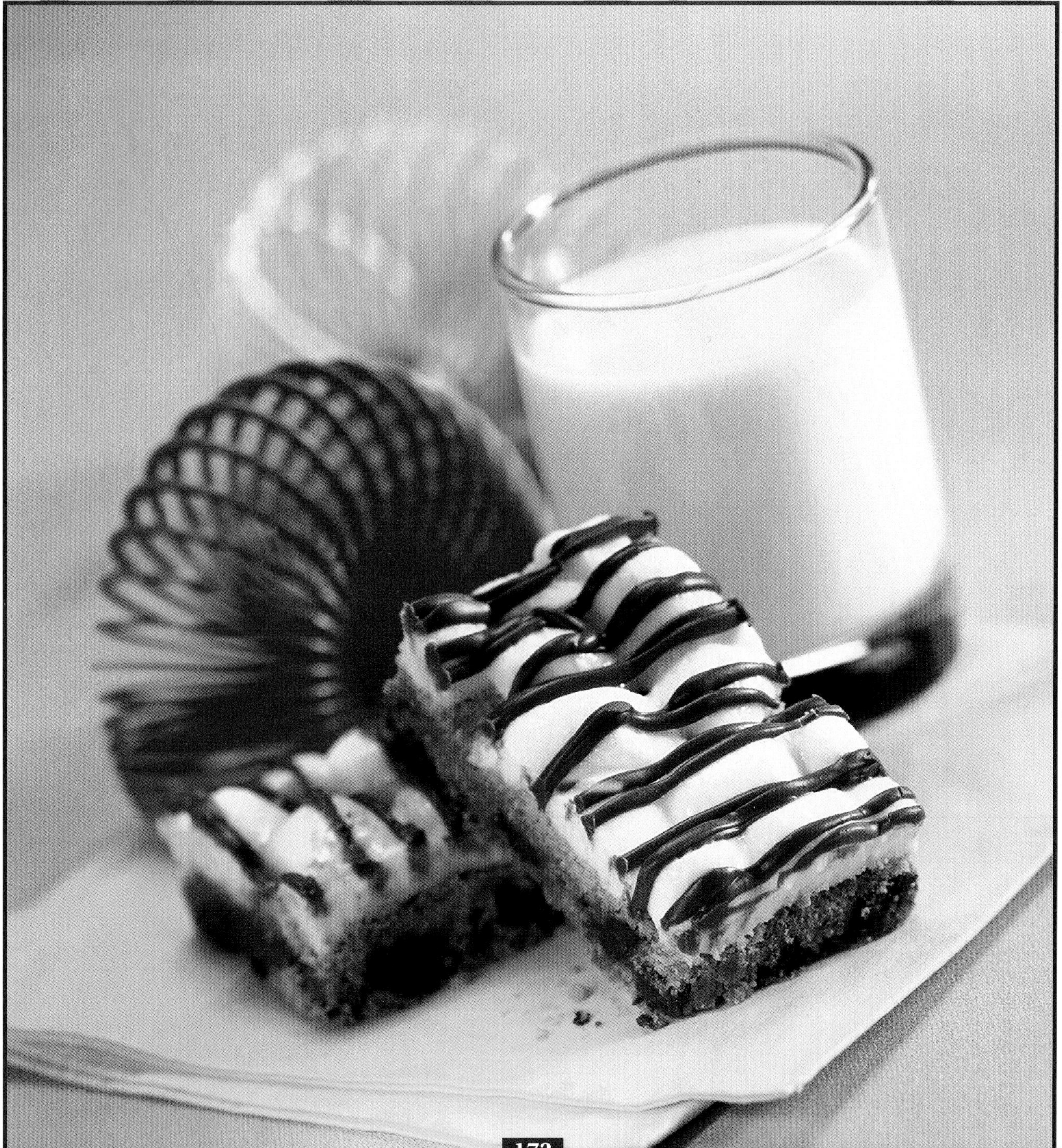

Buried Cherry Bars

1 jar (10 ounces) maraschino cherries

1 package (18¼ ounces) devil's food cake
    mix *without* pudding in the mix

1 cup (2 sticks) butter, melted

1 egg

½ teaspoon almond extract

1½ cups semisweet chocolate chips

¾ cup sweetened condensed milk

½ cup chopped pecans

1. Preheat oven to 350°F. Lightly grease
13×9-inch baking pan. Drain maraschino
cherries, reserving 2 tablespoons juice. Cut
cherries into quarters.

2. Combine cake mix, butter, egg and almond
extract in large bowl; mix well. (Batter will be
very thick.) Spread batter in prepared pan.
Lightly press cherries into batter.

3. Combine chocolate chips and sweetened
condensed milk in small saucepan. Cook over
low heat, stirring constantly, until chocolate
melts. Stir in reserved cherry juice. Spread
chocolate mixture over cherries in pan;
sprinkle with pecans.

4. Bake 35 minutes or until almost set in
center. Cool completely on wire rack.

Makes 24 bars

Irish Flag Cookies

1½ cups all-purpose flour

1 teaspoon baking powder

½ teaspoon salt

¾ cup granulated sugar

¾ cup light brown sugar

½ cup (1 stick) butter, softened

2 eggs

2 teaspoons vanilla

1 package (12 ounces) semisweet
    chocolate chips

Prepared white frosting

Green and orange food coloring

1. Preheat oven to 350°F. Grease 13×9-inch
baking pan. Combine flour, baking powder
and salt in small bowl; set aside.

2. Beat granulated sugar, brown sugar and
butter in large bowl with electric mixer at
medium speed until light and fluffy. Beat in
eggs and vanilla. Add flour mixture. Beat at low
speed until well blended. Stir in chocolate
chips. Spread batter evenly in prepared pan.
Bake 25 to 30 minutes or until golden brown.
Remove pan to wire rack; cool completely. Cut
into 3¼×1½-inch bars.

3. Divide frosting among 3 small bowls. Tint
one with green food coloring and one with
orange. Leave remaining frosting white. Frost
each cookie with one orange stripe, one white
stripe and one green stripe to resemble the
Irish flag. *Makes 2 dozen cookies*

Conversation Heart Cereal Treats

20 large marshmallows

2 tablespoons butter

3 cups frosted oat cereal with marshmallow bits

16 large conversation hearts

1. Line 8- or 9-inch square pan with heavy-duty foil, leaving 2-inch overhang on 2 sides. Generously grease foil or spray with nonstick cooking spray.

2. Heat marshmallows and butter in medium saucepan over medium heat 3 minutes or until melted and smooth, stirring constantly. Remove from heat.

3. Add cereal; stir until completely coated. Spread in prepared pan; press evenly onto bottom using greased rubber spatula. Press heart candies into top of treats while still warm, evenly spacing to allow 1 heart per bar. Let cool 10 minutes. Remove treats from pan using foil. Cut into bars.   *Makes 12 bars*

Prep and Cook Time: 18 minutes

Scotcheroos

Nonstick cooking spray

1½ cups creamy peanut butter

1 cup granulated sugar

1 cup light corn syrup

6 cups toasted rice cereal

1⅔ cups (11-ounce package) NESTLÉ® TOLL HOUSE® Butterscotch Flavored Morsels

1 cup (6 ounces) NESTLÉ® TOLL HOUSE® Semi-Sweet Chocolate Morsels

COAT 13×9-inch baking pan with cooking spray.

COMBINE peanut butter, sugar and corn syrup in large saucepan. Cook over medium-low heat, stirring frequently, until melted. Remove from heat. Add cereal; stir until thoroughly coated. Press onto bottom of prepared baking pan.

MICROWAVE butterscotch morsels and semi-sweet chocolate morsels in large, uncovered, microwave-safe bowl on HIGH (100%) power for 1 minute. STIR. Morsels may retain some of their original shape. If necessary, microwave at additional 10- to 15-second intervals, stirring just until morsels are melted. Spread over cereal mixture.

REFRIGERATE for 15 to 20 minutes or until topping is firm. Cut into bars.
Makes 2½ dozen bars

"Everything but the Kitchen Sink" Bar Cookies

1 package (18 ounces) refrigerated chocolate chip cookie dough
1 jar (7 ounces) marshmallow creme
½ cup creamy peanut butter
1½ cups toasted corn cereal
½ cup miniature candy-coated chocolate pieces

1. Preheat oven to 350°F. Grease 13×9-inch baking pan. Remove dough from wrapper according to package directions.

2. Press dough into prepared baking pan. Bake 13 minutes.

3. Remove baking pan from oven. Drop teaspoonfuls of marshmallow creme and peanut butter over hot cookie base.

4. Bake 1 minute. Carefully spread marshmallow creme and peanut butter over cookie base.

5. Sprinkle cereal and chocolate pieces over melted marshmallow and peanut butter mixture.

6. Bake 7 minutes. Cool completely on wire rack. Cut into 2-inch bars.

Makes 3 dozen bars

PB Berry Bars

2 cups instant oatmeal
½ cup peanut butter
½ cup miniature semisweet chocolate chips, divided
¼ cup canola oil, divided
¼ cup packed brown sugar
1 teaspoon ground cinnamon
¾ cup finely chopped strawberries

1. Heat 12-inch skillet over medium-high heat until hot. Add oatmeal; cook and stir 6 minutes or until lightly brown and fragrant. Remove from skillet and set aside.

2. Mix peanut butter, 5 tablespoons chocolate chips, 2½ tablespoons oil, sugar and cinnamon in skillet. Cook and stir until well blended and thoroughly melted. Remove from heat; add oats and stir until well blended. Press mixture firmly into 9-inch square baking pan with rubber spatula. Freeze 15 minutes. Sprinkle strawberries evenly over crust.

3. Heat remaining chocolate morsels and oil in small saucepan over low heat; stir until completely melted. Drizzle melted chocolate over strawberries. Cover with foil and freeze at least 2 hours.

4. Let stand 10 minutes at room temperature before cutting into squares. Store leftovers in freezer.

Makes 16 servings

Granola Raisin Bars

1 package (18¼ ounces) yellow cake mix
   with pudding in the mix, divided

½ cup (1 stick) butter, melted, divided

1 egg

4 cups granola cereal with raisins

1. Preheat oven to 350°F. Lightly spray
13×9-inch baking pan with nonstick cooking
spray. Reserve ½ cup cake mix; set aside.

2. Combine remaining cake mix, 4 tablespoons
melted butter and egg in large bowl; stir until
well blended. (Dough will be thick and sticky.)
Spoon dough into prepared pan. Cover with
plastic wrap and press dough evenly into pan,
using plastic wrap to keep hands from sticking
to dough.

3. Bake 8 minutes. Meanwhile, combine
reserved cake mix, granola cereal and
remaining 4 tablespoons melted butter in
medium bowl; stir until well blended. Spread
mixture evenly over partially baked bars.

4. Return pan to oven; bake 15 to 20 minutes
or until edges are lightly browned. Cool
completely on wire rack.   *Makes 15 bars*

Peanut Butter Cheesecake Bars

1 package (18¼ ounces) yellow cake mix
   with pudding in the mix

½ cup (1 stick) butter, softened, cut into
   small pieces

2 packages (8 ounces each) cream cheese,
   softened

1 cup chunky peanut butter

3 eggs

1¼ cups sugar

1 cup salted roasted peanuts

   Melted chocolate (optional)

1. Preheat oven to 325°F. Combine cake mix
and butter in large bowl; beat with electric
mixer at medium speed just until crumbly.
Reserve 1 cup mixture. Press remaining
mixture evenly into ungreased 13×9-inch
baking pan to form crust. Bake 10 minutes;
cool on wire rack.

2. Combine cream cheese and peanut butter
in large bowl; beat with electric mixer at
medium speed until fluffy. Beat in eggs,
one at a time, scraping down side of bowl
occasionally. Gradually beat in sugar until
light. Spoon filling over cooled crust.

3. Combine reserved cake mix mixture and
peanuts; spread evenly over filling.

4. Bake 45 minutes or until cake is just set and
knife inserted in center comes out clean. Cool
30 minutes at room temperature. Chill at least
2 hours before serving. Drizzle with melted
chocolate, if desired.   *Makes 24 servings*

Peanut Butter Chips and Jelly Bars

1½ cups all-purpose flour

½ cup sugar

¾ teaspoon baking powder

½ cup (1 stick) cold butter or margarine

1 egg, beaten

¾ cup grape jelly

1⅔ cups (10-ounce package) REESE'S®
Peanut Butter Chips, divided

1. Heat oven to 375°F. Grease 9-inch square baking pan.

2. Stir together flour, sugar and baking powder in large bowl. With pastry blender or two knives, cut in butter until mixture resembles coarse crumbs. Add egg; blend well. Reserve 1 cup mixture; press remaining mixture onto bottom of prepared pan. Stir jelly to soften; spread evenly over crust. Sprinkle 1 cup peanut butter chips over jelly. Stir together reserved crumb mixture with remaining ⅔ cup chips; sprinkle over top.

3. Bake 25 to 30 minutes or until lightly browned. Cool completely in pan on wire rack. Cut into bars.   *Makes about 16 bars*

Tip: For a whimsical twist on this tried-and-true classic, use cookie cutters to cut out shapes for added fun.

Monkey Bars

3 cups miniature marshmallows

½ cup honey

⅓ cup butter

¼ cup peanut butter

2 teaspoons vanilla

¼ teaspoon salt

4 cups crispy rice cereal

2 cups rolled oats, uncooked

½ cup flaked coconut

¼ cup peanuts

Combine marshmallows, honey, butter, peanut butter, vanilla and salt in medium saucepan. Melt marshmallow mixture over low heat, stirring constantly. Combine rice cereal, oats, coconut and peanuts in 13×9×2-inch baking pan. Pour marshmallow mixture over dry ingredients. Mix until thoroughly coated. Press mixture firmly into pan. Cool completely before cutting.   *Makes 2 dozen bars*

Microwave Directions: Microwave marshmallows, honey, butter, peanut butter, vanilla and salt in 2-quart microwave-safe bowl on HIGH 2½ to 3 minutes. Continue as above.

Favorite recipe from **National Honey Board**

The publisher would like to thank the companies and organizations listed below for the use of their recipes and photographs in this publication.

ACH FOOD COMPANIES, INC.
Birds Eye® Foods
Cherry Marketing Institute
Chilean Fresh Fruit Association
Crisco is a registered trademark of The J.M. Smucker Company
Del Monte Corporation
Dole Food Company, Inc.
Eagle Brand® Sweetened Condensed Milk
The Golden Grain Company®
Hebrew National®
Heinz North America
Hershey Foods Corporation
Hillshire Farm®
Hormel Foods, Carapelli USA, LLC and Melting Pot Foods Inc.
Keebler® Company
The Kingsford® Products Co.
Lawry's® Foods
© Mars, Incorporated 2005
MASTERFOODS USA
Mott's® is a registered trademark of Mott's, LLP
National Honey Board
Nestlé USA
Northwest Cherry Growers
Peanut Advisory Board
Reckitt Benckiser Inc.
Sargento® Foods Inc.
Southeast United Dairy Industry Association, Inc.
StarKist Seafood Company
Sun•Maid® Growers of California
Reprinted with permission of Sunkist Growers, Inc.
Texas Peanut Producers Board
Unilever Foods North America
Veg•All®

Index

Index

METRIC CONVERSION CHART

VOLUME MEASUREMENTS (dry)

$1/8$ teaspoon = 0.5 mL
$1/4$ teaspoon = 1 mL
$1/2$ teaspoon = 2 mL
$3/4$ teaspoon = 4 mL
1 teaspoon = 5 mL
1 tablespoon = 15 mL
2 tablespoons = 30 mL
$1/4$ cup = 60 mL
$1/3$ cup = 75 mL
$1/2$ cup = 125 mL
$2/3$ cup = 150 mL
$3/4$ cup = 175 mL
1 cup = 250 mL
2 cups = 1 pint = 500 mL
3 cups = 750 mL
4 cups = 1 quart = 1 L

VOLUME MEASUREMENTS (fluid)

1 fluid ounce (2 tablespoons) = 30 mL
4 fluid ounces ($1/2$ cup) = 125 mL
8 fluid ounces (1 cup) = 250 mL
12 fluid ounces ($1 1/2$ cups) = 375 mL
16 fluid ounces (2 cups) = 500 mL

WEIGHTS (mass)

$1/2$ ounce = 15 g
1 ounce = 30 g
3 ounces = 90 g
4 ounces = 120 g
8 ounces = 225 g
10 ounces = 285 g
12 ounces = 360 g
16 ounces = 1 pound = 450 g

DIMENSIONS

$1/16$ inch = 2 mm
$1/8$ inch = 3 mm
$1/4$ inch = 6 mm
$1/2$ inch = 1.5 cm
$3/4$ inch = 2 cm
1 inch = 2.5 cm

OVEN TEMPERATURES

250°F = 120°C
275°F = 140°C
300°F = 150°C
325°F = 160°C
350°F = 180°C
375°F = 190°C
400°F = 200°C
425°F = 220°C
450°F = 230°C

BAKING PAN SIZES

Utensil	Size in Inches/Quarts	Metric Volume	Size in Centimeters
Baking or Cake Pan (square or rectangular)	$8 \times 8 \times 2$	2 L	$20 \times 20 \times 5$
	$9 \times 9 \times 2$	2.5 L	$23 \times 23 \times 5$
	$12 \times 8 \times 2$	3 L	$30 \times 20 \times 5$
	$13 \times 9 \times 2$	3.5 L	$33 \times 23 \times 5$
Loaf Pan	$8 \times 4 \times 3$	1.5 L	$20 \times 10 \times 7$
	$9 \times 5 \times 3$	2 L	$23 \times 13 \times 7$
Round Layer Cake Pan	$8 \times 1 1/2$	1.2 L	20×4
	$9 \times 1 1/2$	1.5 L	23×4
Pie Plate	$8 \times 1 1/4$	750 mL	20×3
	$9 \times 1 1/4$	1 L	23×3
Baking Dish or Casserole	1 quart	1 L	—
	$1 1/2$ quart	1.5 L	—
	2 quart	2 L	—